Hospice Whispers:
Stories of Life

Rev. Dr. Carla Cheatham

Hospice Whispers: Stories of Life by Carla Cheatham

Front cover initial image by Amy Kappler www.hipposeatingalligators.com
Front cover art by Laura Saintey acrylic painting.
Front cover graphic design by Laura Jenkins www.storyscape.com

"The Day of the Dying," is published with permission of Bernadette Noll who retains the copyright; "Of Course You Feel That Way", is published with permission of Joan Kingery who retains the copyright; "Unexpected Gifts" is published with permission of Rev. Dr. Rodney Bolejack who retains the copyright.

This book includes information from many sources and gathered from many personal experiences. It is published for general reference and is not intended to be a substitute for medical, legal, psychosocial or other professional advice or support services when necessary and appropriate. This book is sold with the understanding that the author copyright owners and publisher disclaim any personal or collective liability, directly or indirectly for advice or information presented within these pages. Although the manuscript has been prepared with utmost care and diligence and every effort made to ensure the completeness of the information herein, author, copyright owners and publisher assume no responsibility for errors, inaccuracies, omissions or inconsistencies. Neither is any liability assumed for damages resulting from the use of the information contained herein. All clients' and patients' names have been changed and identifying details modified to preserve the privacy of patients, clients, their families and/or friends.

Cataloging-in Publication Data
Carla Cheatham

Hospice Whispers: Stories of Life
•Hospice Care II. Palliative Care III. Personal Narratives IV. Terminally Ill Care
R 726.8   362.175 CH

ISBN: 978-0-9966010-0-9

Printed in the United States of America

PRAISE FOR *Hospice Whispers: Stories of Life*
AND AUTHOR CARLA CHEATHAM

What hospice and palliative care staff are saying:

Hospice Whispers is a beautifully written book of stories about the lives of patients and families at life's end. It reminds us that we are all spiritual beings—including the many professionals who provide the care. This book is a great gift to the ever growing field of palliative care and reminds us that much healing and blessing comes in the final chapter of life.

Betty Ferrell PhD, FAAN, FPCN
Professor and Director, Nursing Research,
City of Hope Medical Center

This book is full of personal stories and experiences, which set a great field in which Carla gives the reader insights and teaches about being a Hospice Chaplain. Carla lets us know it's more than OK to be human, to laugh and to cry, not alone, but alongside those we minister to. Carla gives a broader audience the chance to experience this. I think this book would not only be a good read for Hospice Chaplains, but all Chaplains. I can see this being a good thing to read for families entering Hospice too, as they do not know what to expect, but Carla's storytelling will give them some insight, and permission to do as they need, not what they think they should do. Well done Carla.

Kenneth E. Ingram
Chaplain, Heart Hospital of Austin

Awesome Book!

Finally, the words to express what I have always felt! This book totally resonates with me. I cried many tears and found words to express my own pain and grief. I now understand the concept of being not fixing. What a gift!

Yes!

So right on! I am a nurse with Hospice, but all of what makes our clients who they are blends the physical, emotional, and spiritual! I was moved to understand a professional explanation of many situations I have experienced in my work!

Yes, you can work in tough jobs caring for others— and still harve a heart!

At times heart-rending, sometimes half-apologetic, but always boldly honest, this collection of stories does much more than teach about hospice. Author Carla Cheatham is the chaplain I would want at my bedside in any circumstance. I am one myself, but I don't know any who are as comfortable in their own skin and with their own process as she is. Thank you for such a breath of fresh air! I highlighted all over the place, starting with slugging the snot out of a judgmental chaplain. This examination of the spiritual journey at the end-of-life (yours or that of anyone you love) is comforting, clarifying, and completely accepting, no matter what "religion" (or "no religion") you may happen to label yourself. I read it as an Ash Wednesday practice and felt so freed to know that I don't have to fix it; I can't fix it; and I don't GET to fix it. And it's OK.

Loved it.

As a hospice chaplain I could so relate to the stories and the situations, funny and sad, but heartwarming…love it and would recommend to anyone, chaplain or anyone interested in hospice.

What families and other readers are saying:

Hospice Whispers is a must read!

Carla does a wonderful job of describing the "end of life" issues she faced as a Hospice Chaplain. This book made me laugh, cry, and wish I had known more of what she shares before my mom passed away. I recommend *Hospice Whispers: Stories of Life* for anyone who has a parent or loved one who is older than they are... Yes, that means everyone should have a copy of this book in his or her library!

Highly recommend!

Beautifully written without being sappy and overly emotional. I choked back a few tears but mostly had my eyes opened to the process of hospice and the true roles these wonderful providers fill.

Touching and uplifting stories.

This book is very useful for a wider audience than Hospice folks. A dear friend of mine just lost one of her good friends and the book was very insightful in letting me see ways that I could avoid putting my foot in my mouth and how important just being there with her is. Touching and uplifting stories.

Lessens fears…stories of inspirational care for persons of all spiritual paths

Carla's true stories of those transitioning from this life into the next show the indomitable human spirit of all of us. Her stories lessen the fear of those who are transitioning and those who love them. Her willingness to walk a spiritual path in whatever spiritual tradition the dying person has is touching and inspirational. This book is a must read for us all no matter whether we are in our paths in life. You will be blessed by this book.

Hospice Whispers is beautifully written and a true affirmation of life and death

I selected a gem! *Hospice Whispers* is beautifully written and a true affirmation of life and death and what I've experienced in the reality of both. I don't know if I've done more laughing or crying as I've been reading, but I've been learning. I think the learning is what will last in my mind and what will be most important in my life.

Helpful and entertaining!

I found this book very helpful with how I approach/talk with my ageing parents… And, on top of teaching me something, this book was entertaining to read.

And what amazing heartfelt stories they are

I attended a presentation by Chaplain Carla Cheatham in which she told many of these stories. She has written them in her true voice, and what amazing heartfelt stories they are. If you or a loved one have ever considered hospice, I encourage you to read this book. If you have never really considered it, but wondered what it would be like, I encourage you to…read this book.

Check out **Goodreads.com** or **Amazon.com** for more reviews and comments.

Dedication

To all those who contributed to help make this project possible.
We're off to a great start!

To Linda Wiles, my free thinking friend and constant cheerleader.

To my chosen family at "The Hill," who love and
support me in a very special way.

To the original Chaplain Development Committee: Diane, Brandie, Rodney, Linda, Danny, Paul, and Dennis, who share my passion, first gave these
stories a voice, kept me from getting small,
and still howl at the moon with me.

To Larry Farrow and the Texas New Mexico Hospice Organization Board of
Directors, for believing in this rabble-rousing bunch of chaplains and helping start the movement.

To Dr. Marcia Levetown, for honoring me with your trust in so many ways.
I still want to be you when I grow up.

To Spike Gillespie and the Tuesday Night Memoir group, for being my gracious guinea pigs and gentle guides.

To Sheila, who asks the big questions of my heart that give me pause and the
courage to follow the answers,
even when they make my knees shake.

To Cheryl, who told me I could write, and so much more,
and helped me to finally believe it, myself.
I will always love you for that.

A special thank you to Amy Kappler of Hippos Eating Alligators, for giving
me my talisman and allowing me to share the beauty.

To Laura Saintey for capturing the essence so beautifully with
your paint and brush and spirit.

To Laura Jenkins, who connected me with the writing world and designed the
marquee to launch me out into it.

To contributors: Joan Kingery, RN, Rev. Dr. Rodney Bolejack, and Bernadette Noll for sharing their work and wisdom.

To my publishing team at The Authors' Assistant, Mindy Reed and Danielle
Hartman, for your patient guidance, flexibility, encouragement, and sharing
the excitement.

Thanks to each of you for sharing your talents.

Table of Contents

Introduction

I OFTEN JOKE that if you want to suck all the air out of the room at a dinner party, tell folks you work for hospice. They gasp, place their hands to their chests, and say almost in a whisper, "Oh…that must be so hard!" Sometimes they'll tell me their story of hospice, and I appreciate their willingness to share the joys and sorrows of their experiences. Other times, they'll ask questions. Usually, they talk about what "angels" or "special people" hospice workers are. Almost always, the energy significantly changes to a more somber tone.

Then they learn I am a chaplain. Glasses of wine slide surreptitiously behind persons' backs and they begin to use what I call "Sunday School" language about how blessed they are. You can almost see them scrolling through the last 15 minutes of conversation for any "blue" humor or profanity they may have used. This saddens me as the last thing I wish is for my presence to trigger fear or discomfort, but so many have experienced judgment in their lives that I cannot begrudge their reaction.

I'm quick to ask them to relax, and remind them that chaplains are not to judge or preach. We seek to learn what a person's beliefs are and then help them access those beliefs to find as much peace and meaning and comfort as possible. "In fact," I tell them, "if you come across a judgmental chaplain, slap the snot out of them and tell them to find a new job because they have no business being a chaplain!"

So many myths exist about hospice, what it means, and what we do. Combine these misunderstandings with our death-denying culture, a recent development in human history, and you find far too many people wait far too long to access the services that offer so much support. I would like to change that. Just as I want others to feel safe and comfortable with me as a chaplain, I also wish them to understand and embrace the tremendous gifts hospice care can provide patients and families when the time comes that such care is needed.

While most people believe this would be a depressing field of work, it's actually the most rewarding and humbling work I've ever done. Often, it's also the most fun! Contrary to popular thought, the joys far outweigh the sorrows.

The "dying" part of hospice happens in an instant. What we get to be a part of is all that marvelous living that happens until that moment. That is where the good stuff is.

In the hospice field, we say that we don't help people die, we help them live as fully as possible, as long as naturally possible, so they can enjoy every moment possible doing the things they love with dignity, comfort, and peace. With the help of hospice, they get to set their own terms. Illness may have decided how they are going to die, but we get to help them determine how they are going to live, right up to that instant.

Every day, I get to experience life, not death; real, honest, nitty-gritty, gut-wrenching, poignant, joyful, and even hilarious LIFE in all its messiness and mystery, chaos and beauty. I get to watch people find clarity about what really matters to them. The petty is put aside as they focus on what's truly significant: resolving internal and interpersonal issues and struggles. They whisper confessions, give and accept forgiveness, reconcile their faith, find meaning in their life, and pass on the best of themselves to their loved ones.

Of course, it's not always that pretty. I watch greed and bitterness complicate circumstances. I observe persons whose wealth and privilege or intelligence and power have robbed them of the gift of learning to accept powerlessness and disappointment. Having never had to face a hard and fast "No" from life, they often struggle the most with accepting the limitations that illness and death impose on us all.

I also encounter situations in which the living, in struggling with their grief, reveal some of their worst selves. Pre-existing and unresolved family dynamics, mental illness, or addiction issues can become quite amplified when death comes near.

Luckily, these are the proverbial exceptions. All of what I see helps make me a better person every single day, and I guarantee you, I learn more lessons than I could ever teach or preach. In some cases, the lessons are about how I do not want to do this process of living and letting go. More often, I learn how I do want my own process of living to be, both now and in my own "end of life" future.

Those who witness the very end of life process often share with a sense of awe that it is very much like watching birth. They may use different words, but the sentiment is the same—they watch the body labor to let go, and it is often hard work for the body to stop doing what it has always known to do; they experience the suffering and the quiet peace that most often comes in the final moments; they shiver with the feeling of witnessing something intimate and beautiful and mysterious, even sacred; and they hear the reverential silence when the last breath—the final whisper—is released.

This book is about the "gestation period"—the moments leading up to that "birth." People invite hospice workers into their homes and lives at the most precious and precarious of times and let us see them in the most real way. They allow us to walk with them. They tell us their stories. They bring us laughter with their jokes and phenomenal personalities. They share their joys and regrets, tenderness and tears, and eek out slowly and quietly their deepest grief and fears.

They trust us with their physical, emotional, and spiritual struggles and honor us to walk alongside them as a companion, of sorts. In so doing, they teach me about living as I learn to reconcile with death, freeing me to enjoy and reaffirm how precious and precarious each blessed moment is in my life.

The stories shared here are my interpretation of events as I perceived them and the lessons I took from them. Names and details have been changed to protect identities and confidentiality. I hope that you will be inspired, intrigued, challenged and comforted by the whispers that grace my ears every day—that allow me to be present much like a midwife, if you will. Midwife? you may wonder.

The following is a translation from Lao Tzu's *The Tao of Leadership*. It is called "Being a Midwife" and has been deeply important to me since I first began working as a therapist and group facilitator over 20 years ago.

Being A Midwife
by Lao Tzu
The Tao of Leadership (5th century B.C.E.)

The wise leader does not intervene unnecessarily. The leader's presence is felt, but often the group runs itself. Lesser leaders do a lot, say a lot, have followers and form cults.

Even worse ones use fear to energize the group and force to overcome resistance. Only the most dreadful leaders have bad reputations.

Remember that you are facilitating another person's process. It is not your process. Do not intrude. Do not control. Do not force your own needs and insights into the foreground. If you do not trust a person's process, that person will not trust you.

Imagine that you are a MIDWIFE. You are assisting at someone else's birth. Do good without show or fuss. Facilitate what is happening rather than what you think ought to be happening.

If you must take the lead, lead so that the mother is helped yet still free and in charge. When the baby is born, the mother will rightly say: "We did it ourselves."

This reading describes the intention I continually seek to "grow into" when I am invited into another's journey. It reminds me to respect their autonomy, dignity, inherent worth and wisdom.

Just as it was when I worked as a therapist years ago, ethical boundaries dictate that I remember the sacred trust they have placed in me by inviting me into their lives. This is their journey, not mine. Whether anything else needs to happen for them emotionally or spiritually is not for me to decide. I believe there is a power much wiser and greater than me that loves them far more than I ever could, so I need not be in charge or believe that I know what they need or want. I trust each person's process of finding his or her own way.

I am just a temporary visitor, walking alongside them. The gifts and lessons that come from these experiences, and the stories I tell in these pages, are theirs. I simply get to collect them and share them with you. For that, and for all the patients and families who have trusted the stories of their lives to me, I am truly grateful.

Peacefully yours,

Carla

The Tao of Leadership: Lao Tzu's Tao Te Ching Adapted for a New Age [John Heider, 1985] Humanics Ltd., Atlanta, GA p.33

Reclaiming Our Connection with Death

We once were not shielded from death. We faced it when a calf came breech and could not be saved; when we shot at the bird with our slingshot never intending to actually be able to hit it; and when Granddad, who lived with us, died. That's when our uncles and father took the parlor door off its hinges and laid him out on two saw horses and a piece of plywood for folks to come pay their respects and sit with us as we grieved. It was close and personal. We smelled it, touched it. We sat with it and were immersed in the whole experience.

Today, we call kind men and women who, after we give her one last kiss, take Grandmamma out under a pretty felt blanket in a non-descript dark black minivan with tinted windows—even the well-known hearse is now gone from our sight. I believe we are hungry to reconnect with death, others' and our own. We want to be more in touch, literally and figuratively, and hospice is helping to make that happen. It is what will draw us once again to the true spirit of healthcare, and swing the pendulum back from the sterilized and impersonal place we go to when our technological advances launch us further ahead than our wisdom can adequately carry us.

Fortunately, we are coming back to ourselves. Home funerals are becoming more popular. Green cemeteries can be found in many major cities. Comfort with organ donation and cremation are increasing. Even funeral directors are realizing how far removed we've become from death and are opening up to greater involvement from the family. They are making room for members to be present at cremations or finding other ways to bring the family more into the entire experience.

When one of my own relatives died, the family was much more "hands on" with his care than expected. Unfortunately, it was one of those rare hospice stories that was not positive, and we had to provide much more of his care than should normally be necessary. They were understaffed and incredibly slow to respond, often completely failing to call or show up when promised, so we were left out in a very rural area very much on our own medically, emotionally, and spiritually.

One chaplain came and preached at the wife non-stop in lengthy sermon illustrations until she, normally a very polite to the point of being timid woman, asked him to leave her house. The next chaplain was sweet, but conversed little and during the prayer kept calling our loved one, "Thomas." His wife, again breaking her usually excessively respectful ways, finally interrupted the prayer to correct her, "Excuse me, but his name is Frank!" After that, we asked them to not send another chaplain.

I did not work for hospice, yet, but wound up being one of the main ones to change his briefs, bathe him, change his external catheter, monitor his medications, and clean and dress his bedsores. Now that I know how wonderful hospice can be and most often is, I believe that whole story is a large part of what drives me to help make certain that hospice is the best possible experience for patients and families.

Thankfully, that hospice soon folded. There are some things that we only get one chance to do well. Care at the end of life is one of those things, and a community will not continue to support a business that cannot bring the best they have to that care.

We did not know that we could have easily changed hospice providers when they repeatedly failed us. I so wish we had. But now I know to tell others they always have that choice if they find they just can't work with a particular group. Thankfully, that's the exception and not the rule!

Because they provided so little support, and I helped with so much of his hands-on care, I felt that much more responsible when he died, and very protective. It was a challenging situation, and I'm certain I was way too controlling and probably unbearable for the family to deal with. Thankfully, they still loved me.

To let go of him was harder than it might have been otherwise, and I needed to be the one to bathe and dress him one more time. Thankfully, the funeral directors who came were absolutely wonderful. "I don't want to make your jobs harder," I told them, "but I need to do this. You tell me what to do, and I'll do it."

Much to their credit, they stood back, told me what to do, and let me do it, every bit of it. I cried and went through the ritual I needed to do to say goodbye and get to the point where I could let go and let someone else take over his care, down to shutting the door on the van after his gurney had been locked into place. It was almost a decade ago, and I can still see the shiny chrome handle and feel the slick surface of the highly waxed black paint of the door. I said my final goodbye and then handed him over to them.

When family members get a little "crazy" on us I now have much more patience with them because I've been there. I was them, and I know how such stress and grief can bring out both our best and our worst.

I remember everything about that experience, except the faces of the two dark-suited funeral workers who kindly let me do exactly what I needed to do. I wish I could remember and tell them exactly how much that meant to me. So today, I am especially fond of good funeral directors and try to remember to thank them for the caring way they treat families and the respectful way they handle persons who have died.

We lost our ability to hold that space for a long time in the latter part of the twentieth century, but I believe we are getting it back. Over 8,000 "Baby Boomers" are turning 65 years old every day, and this is projected to continue for the next 18 years. They are the most educated consumer cohort to enter end of life care we have ever seen. They got daddies out of the waiting rooms, where they chain-smoked and wore grooves in the tile as they paced back and forth in the 1950s, and into the delivery room. In the 1960s and 70s, they even took birth out of the hospital and into their homes.

Now, I believe they will revolutionize how we do the end of life. Many of you will demand more individualized and patient-centered care. You will require us in the industry to be our best selves, and to find increasingly creative ways to provide superb services to an enormous swell of persons without lapsing back into an industrial-institutional model where we simply warehouse persons until they die. The Boomers, and everyone else who holds us to a higher standard, will help us get this right.

You will help our culture that came to so fear death, to get back in touch with what is a natural part of life. Many in healthcare are weary of unnecessarily heroic medical measures that prolong cost and sometimes "life," but at the expense of quality and comfort and dignity for all involved. Together, we will bring the end of life back to a natural rhythm and balance in which professionals show up to lend support and expertise, while loved ones remain connected and involved for it all. In the end, we will all be the better for it.

What Better Place?

One way we seek to avoid the discomfort we feel with death is to deny or minimize the experience of grief that naturally follows. I cared for one woman in her late eighties for several months and came to know the family well. When she died, the family asked me to officiate at her funeral service and burial.

I met with them beforehand to make plans. I heard more of their stories, laughter, and tears as they talked about the momma and grand-mamma they adored. They were a sweet family, had a deep faith, and an old Southern gentility about them.

The large funeral chapel was packed with longtime friends of the family, fellow church members, and others who were there to support the patient's grown children and grandchildren. I appreciate that it makes funeral directors anxious when services start late. Therefore, I went to find the patient's daughter, a well-tailored and cultured woman in her early sixties, to confirm the family was getting seated so we could begin.

As I walked up to her, she squeezed my hand and arm and let out a relieved sigh, pulling me aside. She thanked me for coming to her at that particular moment. Almost vibrating with emotion, she said, "Chaplain, if one more kind, loving, well-intentioned, good-hearted person tells me my momma is in a better place, I'm gonna slap the shit out of them!"

She breathed for a moment as her emotions caught in her throat and her next words came out less as a threat and more as a childlike plea, "Because what better place is there for my momma than right here beside me?"

Her eyes begged me to understand. She yearned for me to tell her she wasn't wrong. She needed a respite—a space to feel validated. She had no more space to be dismissed by easy and cheap words. She needed me to "get it."

I took her hands and said, "On behalf of all the kind, loving, well-intentioned, good-hearted but misguided people who say stupid things, I am so sorry…and when you slap the shit out of them, tell them you have the chaplain's permission to do so."

She burst out laughing and into tears at the same time. I held her as she sobbed a few moments and got some of the pent up energy out on my shoulder. (My dry cleaner expects mascara, salty tear stains, and snot on the shoulders of my suits and clergy robes given my line of work, so it's no big deal.) Finally, she took a slow, deep, calming breath, straightened her suit, deftly patted her make-up back into absolute perfection without a mirror, and thanked me with an appreciative smile.

As she walked off to find her family and their seats, she looked back over her shoulder and said with a classy smile, "I still may actually do it, so just remember, you said it was ok!"

During the funeral, with her consent, I shared an abbreviated form of that story. Everyone laughed, accepting his or her own well-intended mistakes. I assured them that I understand our need to "make it better" and acknowledged that I've made similar mistakes. I am quite certain I likely will again many times in my life and career. We want to help, and yet sometimes what people need most is—more presence and fewer words.

I reminded them of the stories friends and family had shared about Momma, who was known for her exceedingly generous hospitality. She remembered the foods others liked and their favorites were in her home whenever they visited, even if unannounced! Her welcome to others was quiet and simple, and deeply appreciated because people felt seen and known and understood and cared for.

I encouraged all of us in that huge chapel to dig deep and fill the big shoes Momma had left behind by seeking to practice a similar hospitality by saying less and BE-ing fully present with others more.

It is okay to just sit with the pain that is in front of us and offer it a safe and welcoming space to be. We need do nothing beyond that. We can trust love to fill the spaces when we have no words. Usually, when words fail us, it's a decent sign we probably would be better off not speaking at all! All we must do is find whatever we need inside ourselves to be comfortable enough to do so.

The understanding laughter of the chapel that afternoon seemed to repair the damage and alienation the daughter had felt. It brought a sense of calm and connection to the entire room.

We all know this to be true; I'm telling you nothing that you don't already know. But sometimes, we just need someone to remind us that we can just be and that we don't have to "fix" it. We don't need to, we don't have to, and we don't get to do anything else.

Rachmaninoff

The human brain continues to surprise me. Or maybe it's actually the human spirit that flows around and through the gray matter that frequently leaves me in awe. On an almost daily basis, I hear family members and friends tearfully, regretfully, and angrily talk about the person "who is no longer there" when referring to a patient whose brain no longer works, (at least in the way to which we are accustomed).

For the family member or friend, the way they knew that person may seem "gone," but through my work, I have learned they are often more "there" than we often realize at first glance. In our discomfort, we often look away too quickly to really see. I have been given the privilege of seeing the person who is still there—a person who comes shining through in glimmers and even brilliant flashes.

Recently, a video of a daughter laying beside her mother, a woman experiencing dementia, circulated on social media. As they talk, the woman suddenly remembers her daughter's name, much to the daughters delight and surprise. They exchange sweet, "I love yous" to one another before the video ends. Folks viewed it over and over.

As human beings, we are hungry to be seen, to be known. When loved ones with fully functioning brains aren't able to "see" us, it hurts, and leaves us feeling abandoned and rejected. When someone appears physically fit in most ways and yet his or her brain no longer "knows" us, it is emotionally painful. Our brain knows that theirs is just impaired, but our hearts struggle with the disconnect. For those whose parents were already emotionally or physically abandoning or neglectful of them as children, this loss may tap into old wounds and frustration. The situation dredges up feelings they'd rather not go through all over again. It can certainly complicate the grief process. That isn't to minimize the painful experience for even the most loving and healthy of families when a person slowly loses their ability to "know." Pain is relative. The worst you've experienced is the worst you've experienced, and it all hurts.

When the brain is impacted, the results are difficult to predict, even from day to day. We get fooled into thinking that nothing of the person remains inside them, but every day, I get to see that this is not the case. It may take a little longer for the connection to happen; it may not happen every time; it likely will not happen in the same way. However, if we can focus less on the parts that seemingly aren't "there" and allow ourselves to be with what is there, then that simple shift in perspective can open a door to a new way of being with and seeing them.

The family of one dear woman was glad to share the photo book they had made of her very adventurous life. They spoke of her talents and grace and love. Her proper and dignified nature remained in the way she spoke and carried herself, but many of her talents appeared lost. An accomplished musician, I sang with her whatever songs she could find words for each time I visited, often limited to the chorus of "You Are My Sunshine," which we sang over and over.

Research continues to inform us of the ability of music to persist, long after words are gone. Finding the music that was most important to the person in their younger years can sometimes be the key that unlocks the door of connection. I use my smart phone on a regular basis to find and play the "oldies," often with great response, even if it is just the tapping of a long-stilled foot in time with "Chattanooga Choo Choo."

I found her in the activity room of the skilled nursing facility (what used to be called a "nursing home") that was now her home. A music performance was just ending. I was going to push her in her wheelchair back upstairs to dinner, where we would sing for and with her tablemates until the meal arrived. This produced warm laughter and smiles all around. The musician who had just played was a friend of mine, so I stopped by the piano to say hello.

I left the wheelchair briefly to hug my friend, and when I turned back around, my weekly duet partner had used her feet to push her wheelchair in front of the piano. She plinked around on the keyboard with each index finger, hitting seemingly random notes, almost as if she was trying to pick out a song. I questioned whether this would frustrate her more or be enjoyable, so I waited to see.

It was one of those moments when I lapsed into exactly what I teach others not to do. I smiled and thought, "Oh, isn't that cute," a condescending way to consider a grown adult that can easily lead me to think of them as "less than." That means I am not giving them the respect they are richly due. I was about to relearn a valuable lesson

When she found the notes she wanted, a satisfied smile crossed her face. My friend and I looked on, still smiling sweetly at her. With a regal nod at us, she straightened up to sit taller in her chair, paused, and broke into an almost flawless performance of Rachmaninoff's *Prelude in G Minor.*

Shocked, and delightedly humbled, we stood at the piano and enjoyed the impromptu concert until she finally reached a point that she could not remember. Undaunted, she started over and continued to that point again. She improvised an ending, and we applauded as if the master himself had just performed—her performance was actually quite close to that level of quality.

She gave us a smug smile and said, "That's all, folks!" and gave a swirl of her hand to playfully indicate I was to escort the lady to her dinner.

As I left the facility that evening, I wondered if I should share this moment with her children? Would it bring them joy knowing she had that moment, or sadness they had missed it? I trust others with the truth, as it's not my job to think that I know better than they what they can handle. Besides, the process of loving someone through the various forms that dementia may take is, by nature, a pretty bittersweet undertaking. (Note: Dementia itself is not a disease, but a cluster of symptoms that can arise from various diseases or injuries)

I decided to share, and as is often the case, it gave them a chance to process through a bit more of their grief. They were glad for her, sad for themselves, and tearfully relived memories of thousands of hours over their childhoods, listening to their mother play on their great-grandmother's old upright piano. They laughed, they cried, and they found their way, as people usually do.

"I'm sad I missed it," said one daughter, "but you know, it also helps in some weird way for me to hear that the mother I've known really is still in there somewhere, even if she can't show it to us much of the time. I'm glad you told us."

I've always resented the bittersweet—movie endings, songs, situations. For chocolate, it's ok, but overall, there's enough bitter in the world. I prefer to simply have the sweet. And don't we all? But that isn't what life gives us, and I can resent the bitter and miss the sweet, or I can shift my perspective just a bit and soak it all in, feeling gratitude for all of it—however and whenever it comes in this messy ride called Life.

A Familiar Tune

The nurse case manager told me she had dementia. One morning, I went to visit her in the skilled nursing facility where she lived. I planned to arrive after breakfast because I didn't want to distract her from eating. But I wanted to conclude the visit before her shower, which I knew would exhaust her and leave her sleeping the rest of the morning. The nurse and her daughter had both shared with me that mornings seemed to be the best time for her.

She was largely non-verbal, according to family and the facility staff who cared for her 24/7 and knew her well. On my initial visit, I found her sitting alone in the dining room in her wheelchair, pushing food around on her plate with her spoon. She was humming. I took a step into the room, but remained quiet. I stood behind her right shoulder, so as to not disturb what appeared to be a contented moment.

I waited. And then, I recognized the tune, "Take Me Out to the Ballgame"! I walked further into the room and stood a few feet away, listening and amazed to hear her make sound. I should not have been surprised. Again, research shows that music is often one of the last pieces of our memory to leave us, even when our brains are challenged by trauma or disease. I smiled to hear her voice hum the phrase: "Buy me some peanuts and cracker jacks..."

Suddenly, she stopped humming mid-song. I waited, but when she didn't continue after several breathless moments, I took a few slow steps forward and further to her right, so as to not startle her, and picked up where she left off, humming the next phrase—"I don't care if we never get back..."

I knelt down. When I stopped humming, she turned toward me, leaning back a bit as if to ask, "Who are you?!"

She appraised me for a long moment, eyebrows creeping into her well-coifed hairline. I remained at eye level, a less intimidating position to someone with dementia, (and to anyone seated, really), and smiled my gentlest smile.

I breathed slowly and attempted to exude peace and compassion toward her. As a stranger, I did not want to seem threatening as I entered into her space. It can be easy to forget that persons with dementia live in a world that is often confusing and frightening and that they deserve slow, patient, calm approaches and interactions to feel safe and respected.

Her brow relaxed as she sat up straight, still facing me, then raised her head and hummed the next line—"Oh it's root, root, root for the home team…"

Then she stopped, leaned toward me, and raised one eyebrow, looking straight at me with a slight, almost challenging, smirk, and waited!

I hummed, "if they don't win it's a shame…" I stopped, leaned toward her, returned the smirk and raised eyebrow, and waited, as well.

She broke into a wide, full-on grin and lifted her arthritis-curled hands to conduct us both as we hummed together, "For it's one, two, three strikes you're out at the ooooollld, baaalllllll, gaaaaaammmmme!"

We each laughed and clapped our hands as she let out a cheer. She apparently had accepted me, so I moved to kneel in front of her. Finally, she stopped her applause and launched into "BAP ba-da DAA dup," as in, "Shave and a hair cut" and then pointed at me, to which I replied, "dunt DUNT."

It became our first conversation, and was the start of a great relationship.

It is easy to assume that persons who are no longer able to communicate with us in ways we are accustomed to or ways that are easy for us to quickly understand, are no longer there. Sometimes it just takes more patience, more slowness, and more creative ways of looking to really see the person who is still there. It's just in a different way. When we can move past our discomfort with "what is no longer" and embrace "what still is," oh the music we can find.

I had learned from her family that for decades she was the pianist and organist at her church. I learned what some of her favorite hymns were and, as I sang them, she played "air piano," then clapped and cheered after we finished our songs. I never heard her say a word, but we knew how to communicate in a way that was familiar, and life-giving, to us both.

Of Course You Feel That Way

I remember well the look I've seen a hundred times on a spouse or child's face the first time their loved one with dementia no longer recognizes them. No amount of gentle preparation can truly get a person ready for that day.

As the inner world of dementia shifts, often back into long-stored memories, Mom may believe herself to be decades younger than her actual age. In her confusion, she may begin to mistake her daughter for her sister, the child's aunt. Because familiarity can breed comfort and connection, Dad may call caregivers by the name the patient used for his mother or spouse. Sometimes, a person with dementia may not know their loved one's face, but on some level will know that they should know them. Their visage may light up as they delightedly greet their visitor, but after a time it is evident that the name and face escape them.

The impact is often the same as family members, deflated, say, "Dad didn't really know me today," or, "Jim thought I was his nurse," or, "She didn't even try to figure out who I was today." It can feel devastating to be seen, but not known.

Sometimes, a photograph from childhood may be helpful if it corresponds to the time the patient is connected to in their long-term memory banks. The photo may help a patient make the connection between the face of their young child on paper and the unfamiliar grown-up standing in front of them. Although this may help, it cannot make up for the sense of loss that can arise from feeling disconnected from someone you know so intimately. It is heartbreaking when someone you love no longer knows the current you.

When this phase comes to pass, it can be difficult for family members to continue to visit, saying:

"Why do I bother? He doesn't recognize me, anyway!"

"She never remembers my visit from just two days earlier."

"She is angry at me because she thinks I haven't been here to see her."

"I wonder if it does more harm than good for me to even visit."

When family members express this distress, it is important to remind them of research, which indicates that after cognitive memory of an event is gone, persons with dementia may still experience the emotions elicited long afterward (Guzmán-Vélez, et al, Cognitive and Behavioral Neurology September, 2014). It may significantly help family members to know that their visits can make a positive difference and are not a waste of time.

Loved ones are grappling with a myriad of emotions, some of them are difficult to admit such as: "I don't know how much longer I can keep putting myself through this. That's not my wife anymore. It's awful!" Or even, "I wish he would just go ahead and die and end this misery."

Even as these words are spoken, the guilt arises:

"Listen to me, how selfish can I be? How could I ever abandon her?"

"People must think I'm horrid to not be here every day. How heartless am I? It's not like it's his fault."

It is completely normal to want to avoid pain. Sometimes, it can be a warning sign that taking a step back is the sane and caring thing to do for everyone involved. "This is a marathon, not a sprint," we often remind families. "You're allowed to keep some reserves in your tank so you don't burnout before this race is over."

In fact, it is critical that family caregivers find a way to avail themselves of good self-care. Research tells us caregivers are substantially more likely to suffer from depression, anxiety, autoimmune diseases, etc., and may experience an accelerated aging of their immune system (Bennett, Fagundes, and Kiecolt Glaser in Immunosenescence, © Springer Science+Business Media NewYork 2013). Similarly, loved ones are found to be up to 63% more likely to die if they experience the caregiving as a strain (Schulz and Beach, JAMA, 1999). Sacrificing ourselves for those we love serves no one.

The balancing act between self-care and support for an ailing family member is an art that no one can define for another person. Each person must find his or her own way—but finding a sane way is a must. The desire to care for a loved one can easily slide from well-intended responsibility and love into running ourselves absolutely ragged; sometimes out of necessity and other times as a means of avoiding our feelings of grief.

As staff members, we spend as much time as anything else we do normalizing caregivers' feelings and encouraging them to be gentle with themselves. We validate them with: "Of course you feel that way!" We even give families permission to not HAVE to visit so much. "Find the pace that works well for you, so that when you do visit you have something to give him and you go home with something left for yourself and the family waiting for you there."

Simply acknowledging the doubts, frustrations, anguish and fears; and allowing them the feelings, to be seen, accepted, and even normalized by others, can help tremendously. Those aren't burdens anyone should have to carry alone.

The trap we as professionals can fall into is when we want to fix, or at the least, lessen loved ones' grief. We want to help them move more quickly through the grief process as they watch their family member decline. We want to make it all better. Of course we do, and once again we must realize that grief is a journey for which there is no shortcut. The only way out is through.

We show support by educating and sharing what we know from research and experience. We sit with them as they sit with their grief. We wait and watch and hope for moments of connection, which sometimes occur, and provide a few minutes of reprieve from the sadness. And that is why we can keep coming back to do this work each day.

We are not alone in this work. We must reach out to others as well as seek support from others in our community. There is a passion we who do this work bring with us, which carries us through the challenges with a sense of grace and fierce protection of patients and families. When we recognize each other, it helps to feel reminded that we aren't (excessively) bizarre, but have others who understand us, and our common work. Joan Kingery exemplifies this point.

I met Joan Kingery years ago through my work with the Texas New Mexico Hospice Organization. Joan is a hospice nurse who now works as a clinical manager for a small hospice. When we met, it was clear I had met a kindred spirit. Joan and I have shared numerous stories of patients and families who touched us, confounded us, and pushed us to grow. With her permission, I'll share one with you here:

Big John

His life had been spent behind a lens, capturing familiar moments amongst families; waiting for that moment when the shutter would find that one look or smile or tilt of the head that spoke of who they really were with one another.

A very gentle man, he loved his family dearly. He saw them. He knew them. Their love was imprinted in his memory, even as it failed. At first, he would confuse staff members for his wife, and replay daily conversations with her through them about worries over household items that needed repair and errands that needed to be run.

Though he could not remember her face or name, he still felt compelled to care for her as the provider in the family, as he had always been. His tender familiarity with them in those moments clearly displayed the affection he and his wife had long shared. The caregivers reassured him that all the concerns he expressed were being handled.

When the time came that he no longer expressed that same familiarity toward his family members when they visited, it was devastating for them. They struggled with resentment that he expressed this connection with the nurses, but not with his own wife and children. The hospice staff assured the family that he was "still there" and still knew them on some deep level, even though he wasn't able to express it.

"Your touch, that connection, that love is familiar to him even though he does not know your name. He knows your love," Joan gently reminded them.

When the family finally admitted their struggles to Joan and the other members of her hospice team, they were quite embarrassed, but felt relieved when they found absolutely no judgment of their feelings—only acknowledgement and support, "Of course you feel that way! Most people do."

On his last night in this world, everyone—family and staff—were gathered around. His breathing made it clear that death was near. His wife, their kids, and the hospice staff were sprawled around the furniture and floor at his bedside in the facility where he lived. They all knew they needed sleep, and finally agreed it felt right to say their goodbyes and leave for the night.

Whether to stay or go in such moments can often be a hard decision for family. We share our experience with them that families may sit vigil around the clock for days on end, and the patient may wait for that one moment when their loved one steps out into the hallway to speak to a doctor, goes to the bathroom, or falls asleep in the chair beside the bed.

Some patients wait until everyone is around. Others wait until they are alone. Nothing can change that. The saying in the industry is often that a disease process may choose the time of someone's death, but the patient chooses their moment. Families must, again, find what feels right to them and try to avoid feeling guilty for: "not being there" when someone dies. It clearly isn't up to us.

So they decided it was time to let him have space, and allow themselves to rest. The staff made their way out of the room first to give the family privacy. Joan leaned over him, took his face in her hands, thanked him for what he had meant to her, and said goodbye.

John's wife was the last to lean over him, "Honey, I'm going home to get some sleep. I love you, sweetheart." Joan watched from the doorway as John, without ever opening his eyes, turned his head toward his beloved and to her great surprise and delight puckered up his lips to her for one last kiss.

The man who, for months, had no longer brightened as his wife entered or showed any glimpse of recognition of her, had a moment in which her scent, her voice, her touch, her love…something of that was still familiar to him…and he responded to her as he had for decades throughout their lives together. Shortly before his last breath, he knew who she was, even though he did not know her name. This gesture reminded her that he did know her and still loved her. Something of her was still familiar to him, and they got to say their goodbyes one last time.

It doesn't always happen this way. I hesitate to write it just as we hesitate to tell families about "rallies." We fear setting them up for disappointment if the patient doesn't have a burst of energy right before they die. We don't want them to wonder what was wrong about their love or connection that they "didn't warrant" such a moment.

But we also don't want persons to mistake a rally as a healing of some sort and be given false hope if it happens. Nor do we want them to miss the puckering of lips for one last kiss, so we present the possibility.

We wait for moments. Sometimes they come. Sometimes, they never do. But when they do come, we hope we have prepared the family well enough so that, if possible, they may have a moment of grace in which to capture them.

Joan Kingery is a seasoned hospice nurse who now serves as the Director of Clinical Services for a small non-profit hospice in Texas. Over the course of our friendship, she has shared her passion for this work, the stories that have touched her deeply, and the lessons they have taught her. I am eternally grateful for her tender heart and her willingness to share it with patients, families, and with me.

Well, I Guess That's Dad

"**A**w hell, chaplain. I don't know." His eyes were closed as he lay in bed. Then he turned his head toward me, opened one eye in a tired squint and said, "But I tell you what, when I get there, I'll call you and tell you all about it."

He was a dear and funny man, and as his family had told me, he had a sharp and dry sense of humor. The disease that struck his liver quickly and aggressively turned his skin, already darkened by his Hispanic heritage and years of working as a construction foreman in the sun, a deep shade of green-gray.

It also left him completely exhausted.

He intentionally reserved most of his energy for his grandkids, and we respected that wish. Our entire team timed our visits, spread them out, and kept them short to protect what little gas he had left in his tank for the six little bodies that exploded from the yellow bus each afternoon at 4:08 p.m. They were his much-beloved grandkids and they adored him in return. They launched themselves onto Grandpa's king-sized bed each afternoon at 4:09 p.m. and the love-fest began.

They told him animatedly about their days, showed him pictures of cows drawn in purple crayon with pink skies and orange trees, and crumpled tests pulled from the bottom of their book bags with a smiley face and "A+" written on them. Revived by their presence, and his own cussed determination, he oo-ed and ah-ed and hung on their every word, as did they on his.

The youngest stopped from time to time and looked at him silently for a long moment, the little wheels in her head clearly turning. Eventually, she would reach up to touch the skin of his rough cheek, flushed into a strange-to-her color with the various toxins his body could no longer process.

She has just turned five, and she knew something was wrong, but it was taking some time for her to digest it. He said nothing. He just let her be with him and her thoughts. He gave her open space, intuitively knowing he could trust her to ask what she needed to when she was ready.

Children do that. They handle information and emotions as much as they are developmentally able in the moment, and then usually move on, back into the world, as they know it. Eventually, age and experience grant them a greater ability to handle processing an event, even one long past, on a deeper level. We can usually trust them to guide us. Like so many other things in life, we just get to provide an open presence, and they will let us know what they need.

I had been called in because the grandkids had finally begun asking questions. We referred them to a local non-profit that provides grief counseling to children whose loved ones are ill. In the mean time, I was there to hear their concerns and confusion, and then help the grown-ups trust themselves to answer such big questions coming from such tiny and seemingly fragile creatures.

They wanted a chaplain because, though they had a close relationship with their priest and parish, the kids' questions were about what was happening medically, what to expect in the coming days of Grandpa's life, and the afterlife. I am certain their priest could have handled the latter topic just fine, but having a specialist who answers all of these questions every single day is a great resource to have in addition to one's own clergy.

Leaders of faith communities deal with sickness and death as one small part of their ministry, which involves the wearing of so many other hats. This is the only hat we chaplains wear. Thankfully, most clergy understand this and do not feel territorial as they realize we chaplains are just one more person coming to love on their congregant, not to take his or her place as their faith leader.

Just before the kids came home, I met with the patient, his spouse, and their grown children who were all piled on and around the huge bed in the master suite of their home. This is where he wanted to be until he died. I sat on a chair next to his head, so he wouldn't have to strain to speak too loudly. My first goal was to learn what they thought about a life after this one, if they believed in an afterlife.

When asked honestly, and with a clear indication that their answer will not be judged, a lot of persons, even the most religiously devout, will admit to either not believing in an afterlife or having serious doubts about it.

Although I knew they were Catholic, that told me only so much about what it meant to them to be Catholic. I could assume, but we know where that takes us. (I make an ass out of myself regularly enough; I don't need to borrow opportunities).

I asked each family member, starting with Dad/Grandpa, what he or she believed and what they wanted to teach their children. "What do you believe it will be like when you step from this life into the next, if you believe in life after this one?"

And thus came his classic line, "Aw hell, Chaplain. I don't know. But I tell you what, when I get there, I'll call you and tell you all about it."

The family laughed at his good-natured admission of uncertainty. They all spoke of their hopes and prayers and dreams and wishes of what might lie ahead for him—the best fishing holes, already scoped out by his previously deceased best friend; a hot fresh cup of his momma's coffee, which his wife admitted she still couldn't top after 40 years of marriage; maybe watching out over his "babies" as he called them, the kids, their spouses, and grandkids alike from oldest to youngest.

I offered suggestions for responding to the children's worries and questions. I validated their concerns about talking with the kids. This is one thing we really don't want to mess up. It's easier than it may seem, however.

We don't use euphemisms with kids. Telling them someone got "sick" or "tired" or "went to sleep" or "went on a trip" will only scare the heeby-geebies out of them the next time they or someone they love gets sick, tired, or travels. Good luck with bedtime after making that mistake!

Otherwise, short, simple, clear, direct answers are best. Let them draw. Let them talk. Let them play. That's how they process. Again, trust your instincts—you know your children well. Follow their wisdom, too. Let them tell you what they need and want to know.

We processed more of their own feelings, since children take their cues from us, in many ways. The greatest way we can help them is to be in a good place ourselves, and model healthy grieving. They laughed. They cried. They sat in silence. And finally, we prayed, briefly because he was fading, and 4:08 p.m. was fast approaching.

As the last nose was blown, tear wiped, and hug given, the honking horn gave but a moment's notice before the door burst open and six wiggling and giggling dynamos virtually flew from the front door to Grandpa. In that moment, his eyes were bright, though a deep yellow, and wide open for his babies.

I sat with the family as they waited for the questions that did eventually come in the lull after the initial excitement of coming home and coming down from another adventure-filled day. They explained who I was and that I was there to help answer questions.

With Grandma's warm chocolate chip cookies and cold glasses of milk to wash them down, there was even more silence and pause in which to ponder what they wanted to ask. As the questions floated out in bits and pieces, I nodded encouragement to the grown-ups who responded. They did a beautiful job, as I trusted they would, at being with these little ones they knew and loved so well.

Afterward, the family members expressed relief and greater comfort at being able to handle the kids' questions and concerns on their own. Wisely, the kids would still be going to the grief-counseling program. They agreed to call me when they needed any other support.

I guess I could have guessed at what happened next. We like to wrap up details if we can before we die. The things most important to us seem necessary to clean up or "tuck in" before we can let go. Apparently, this was his last.

I received a call at 4:31p.m. the next day. He stayed awake for one more door-bursting entrance, one more round of hugs and giggles and kisses and "show and tell" about their day. Then, he drifted sweetly into his last breaths, surrounded by his beloved wife and his babies.

Luckily, I was moments away and arrived only moments before our nurse. She had to come to officially "pronounce" his death for legal purposes so the attending physician could legally sign the death certificate.

He had already received final communion and the anointing of the sick (often called "last rights"). The priest was caught on the far side of the city in rush-hour traffic and the deacon was out of town. So my presence to say prayers was requested.

As we waited for in-town family to come over to say "one last good-bye," and for the funeral home to arrive to care for him, the family wanted to say one last prayer with just them, before it got too hectic.

Now, "just" them and "too hectic" were relative terms since wife and all the "babies" came to a total of 36 people in the room. They gathered around Dad/Grandpa, snuggled up to him on the bed, circled around it. They held hands or touched him and each other in some way—we prayed.

I was about halfway through when the phone rang. Now, knowing the high esteem with which many Catholics hold the priesthood, I didn't want them to not answer it out of respect for me or the prayer if it was the funeral home or a family member. So I paused.

And in that pause, the wife said, as the ring echoed in the distance, "Well, I guess that's Dad!"

The entire room lost it, breaking into laughter through the sniffles and tears. It was a most appropriate memorial to the man with the quick wit and gentle heart who lived and ultimately died exactly where and how he wanted.

Big Momma

Their parents all had some combination of struggles with mental health and substance abuse disorders. As a result, their grandmother, whom they called Big Momma, had raised all of them. Now she was dying. The one solid space of security, attachment, and comfort in their lives was now also going away.

Their parents had little to no contact with them, and what presence they did provide wasn't helpful; instead it proved to be more disruptive. Twice, the skilled nursing facility where she lived had to call the police because of fights and disruptions from young family members. They did not understand the dying process and demanded actions contrary to the patient's written directive to her physicians regarding what she did and did not want in terms of aggressive treatments.

I knew Big Momma liked to sing. In our time together, she always wanted 1) a Sprite "with lots of that good (a.k.a. crushed) ice" and 2) to sing the spirituals that gave her reassurance that G-d was caring for her and would bring her, in her words, "safely home."

When she died, her grown grandbabies were over-wrought. Their parents, or any grown-ups who could have provided these twenty-something youngsters with comfort and support, were once again unable to be present for them. So they grieved the way they knew how, the way their experience and culture gave them as the appropriate way to get out the energy of their grief and show they cared.

It's what worked for them. It was loud. It seemed violent, at least to those unfamiliar to such ways of emoting. It scared many of the residents and the staff. As I entered, the charge nurse was picking up the phone to call the police. I asked her to give me five minutes. Thankfully, she put the phone back down. Sometimes, carrying the "G-d card" has its advantages.

I work hard to develop good relationships with not only patients and families, but also the staff. The staff is made up of good people who want to help, but they could not allow such a disturbance, which was terrifying the other residents. As I walked down the hall, Big Momma's friends and neighbors on her hallway were closing their doors and avoiding paying last respects to her because the noise and energy of her grandchildren's grief. How they were expressing it was too scary and disturbing for them.

I approached the oldest male cousin, the patriarch of Big Momma's grandbabies. He knew me and knew how much I "loved on" Big Momma. He'd seen me tuck her in, give her a Sprite with "that good ice," and sing her favorite gospel songs with and to her.

I'd always respected his place as the de facto head of his family of young cousins. But today, I saw him as he must have looked as a small child, with tears making tracks down his emotion-swollen cheeks and lines of unwiped mucous smeared from his upper lip across his face toward his ear as he stood in the doorway of her room. He looked at her silent chest under her favorite afghan and wailed openly.

He looked as if he was four years old, lost and alone. He turned pleadingly to me as I walked up. I could tell they were begging for a grown-up to hold space for them and reassure them it was all going to be ok.

It's a tenuous space to hold—respecting an adult's dignity when they are shaken to their core. In that moment they don't want to be the grown-up in the room. I learned this from a man who wept as he stood outside his mother's room—she had just died, "No matter how old you are, when your parent dies, you feel like you're five years old and all you want is your mommy." He was 84. His mother was 103.

But the uncontained wailing and shouting in Big Momma's room and the hallway around it was about to cause a major disruption to their grief. I wanted to avoid any police involvement, although I knew the charge nurse wanted to call them to restore order.

As I walked the last couple of steps, the young, moaning and crying patriarch pushed out of the doorway with force and charged across the hallway. He threw himself hard against the opposite wall in angst. He was about to turn and move on down the hall, fists raised as if he was looking for something to hit, when I made a decision.

I'm generally mindful of how and when I place my hands on patients or family members, but I took a gamble that our trust and connection were great enough, and that my instinct was guiding me well. I intercepted him before he went down the hall and gently but firmly put one hand on his chest. With my free hand, I took his softly in mine. Then I walked him back to the wall he had just willingly crashed into.

I can simultaneously exude authority while sending out compassion with every cell of my being. I called on that skill, seeking to make it clear to him I wanted nothing more than to love and help him and his 15 or so cousins who were spilling out of Big Momma's room.

When he accepted that gesture, I slid the hand on his chest up to his cheek, cupping it in a way I assumed she must have, and quietly said, "I know you need to get it out. I don't want to take a bit of that away from you. But you're scaring your Big Momma's friends, and I know you don't want to do that."

His breath and sobs came out in great heaves.

"Will you sing with me?" I asked. "Sing as loud as you need to. And we'll help send Big Momma safely home together—you, me, your cousins, and her friends?" I started singing one of her favorites, loudly, at the top of my lungs, and then turned to her other grandchildren, whom I knew also knew the songs they had heard all their lives in Big Momma's kitchen and her church. Tentatively at first, and slowly with more feeling, they sang.

Then, as I'd hoped, they took the lead. Instead of moving away from the family over-flowing into the hallway from Big Momma's room, the residents, and even the staff, moved toward them. Doors to the other patients' rooms opened, and they came down the hall toward us in wheelchairs, on walkers, and in nursing home uniforms.

Some sang along if they knew the words. Others just shook hands and hugged necks and gave their condolences. And it was loud. And it was beautiful. And it was just what everyone needed.

The ways we express our grief are varied, but the pain underneath it is universal. What we get to find is our own voice in helping others find theirs in a way that causes less harm and more healing.

That is why I tell staff in training: "If this ever happens to you and you try this approach and get decked and knocked to the floor, please don't blame me. Don't try to mimic me. What works for me and what comes to me in a moment may or may not be what works for you or suits your personality. I've tried to use others' approaches in my work. Sometimes it went beautifully. Sometimes it was disastrous for all involved. I've made, and continue to make, many mistakes in this work of being with those who are living, and grieving, and finding their way, because I am also finding mine! I trust you will find yours."

We all must be willing to think outside the box and get past our cultural norms, experiences, views, or what we think we know. I challenge you to be secure enough in your own skin to be able to think clearly and allow Spirit, or whatever is greater than you that you believe in, to show up in and through you. In those moments when auto-pilot may tell us to go ahead and call the police, to chastise the family and try to calm them down, to make them fit what's comfortable for us and others, rather than what they truly need, stop, listen, and let Grace guide you.

I did ask the family to adjust, but I found a way to do so that allowed them to express what they needed and in a way not only familiar to them, but also in a way that the residents and staff could accept without calling the police. If the police had intervened, their grief would only have been complicated by anger and resentment. We certainly do not want to perpetuate that in our society.

In the Hebrew scripture, Psalm 30:11-12, we read:
You have turned my mourning into dancing; you have taken off my sackcloth and clothed me with joy, so that my soul may praise you and not be silent. O Lord my G-d, I will give thanks to you forever.

A subtle shift is sometimes all that is needed to find a common and healing ground in the midst of pain. An invitation to a new way is what we can offer, but only with the greatest respect for the needs of all involved. Remember, as hospice workers, volunteers and even simply as friends, we are the advocates for what the patient and family need.

When persons are sick or grieving, their voices may be weak from fatigue or pain. They do not need us to speak for them; they deserve us to listen even more closely, so we can help translate to a world who may not be comfortable with or able to hear the way that pain or need is being expressed. We make room for them to be heard.

Those in pain deserve nothing less.

The Day of the Dying

I first heard Bernadette Noll share her experience at a literary event hosted by a mutual friend. It captured my heart immediately and I knew I wanted to share it in this book. Let me preface by saying that research continues to show that the vast majority of persons want to die at home; well over 90% in some surveys. However, only around half are able to do so. The myriad reasons behind this desire to be home are beautifully illustrated in the story below.

The natural ebb and flow of life swirls all around this poignantly written piece, highlighting the precious moments that can be shared as death washes into our midst. Bernadette told me, "Bringing him home was the best thing ever. It wasn't like at the hospital where they treat death as an emergency. At home, we could be more real and accept that this was part of life and there was no emergency."

She also shared of her mom's grief journey, "She was beating herself up, saying she should have said more, should have done this or that. But when she went back to this story I wrote again and again she realized that it was all absolutely perfect!"

From here, I'll let this story speak for itself, but hope that it helps us all perhaps never again…think of death as scary.

The Day of the Dying

In the hospital I asked him, "Any regrets, Dad?" He had just gotten the news a few days prior that his cancer was back with a vengeance and had spread into his marrow. The prognosis was weeks to months.

He pondered the question a minute, "I just wish I had been able to run the 400 hurdles," he sighed. "But they didn't have that event back then." A few days later we brought him home to die.

Dying at home meant life continued around him and was not paused in that lethargic, sickbay way. Meals could be eaten at normal times, children could play instead of having to sit, waiting idly, and sleep could actually take place at night without the buzzers and beeps of the hospital halls and the constant awakenings to find out if one is sleeping okay.

I was there for a visit at first; all the family was there. As the time came to leave, I decided to stay—it was summer, my parents' house was big, my kids were little, and we had nowhere we needed to be. Living far away had been my burden all these years, but now it felt my reward in that it gave me time again in my parents' house—nighttime swims in the lake with my mom, bedtime backrubs for my dying dad, quiet moments with him without the weight of visiting hour conversations, and intimate candle lit talks on the deck with various visiting sisters and brothers. When my brother was leaving after a weeklong visit, he asked if I didn't feel burdened having to stay. "No," in fact I felt gifted.

Right after the news of his fate, my dad called the reservoir where he had worked in water supply for over fifty years. "I'm dying," he told them. "And if you have any questions, now is the time to ask." He knew, as did they, that in addition to the facts of the water and the dams and the methods, he had the history and the lore and other wisdom not in any books or files. A select few came and were loaded up with stories, maps, and experience.

Conversations were lucid and bright, shortened only by his physical exhaustion and when he was finished, he dismissed his guests clearly and succinctly: "Okay, thanks for coming. It's time to say goodbye," he'd dictate. As each person left, they cried and hugged us, sorry for what they were losing, grateful for what they had received.

Several days before the very end, my dad's silence lengthened; he had said what he wanted to say and so had we and we didn't want to saddle him repeatedly with our thoughts of being left behind. My mom would ponder this later, wondering if she could have/should have said more, forgetting that in the end he was already departing, his spirit and his soul already taking leave and heading for the celestial sphere.

On his last day and night he was physically spent, unable to use those same legs that longed to hurdle. The visiting nurse had brought him a catheter condom, the very first condom he would ever wear. That night as my mom and I were settling him in for sleep, the catheter got caught and pulled off. "Oh no," exclaimed my mom. "The visiting nurse put that on. I don't know how to use those things."

"I do," I assured her, smiling.

My dad laid his head back upon the pillow and closed his eyes as I struggled with the medically jerry-rigged prophylactic; all of us aware of a lifetime of modesty wiped out with one terminal illness. Trying hard to be gentle and even harder not to bawl at his incapacity at the end of a very capable lifetime, I got the thing rolled out and he smiled his 76-year-old, trademark, I've-got-a-joke-coming smile. "I don't want to get your mother pregnant and then leave her," he chuckled, still with eyes closed.

His weakness was increasing now by the hour. That morning he stood. That afternoon he sat. That evening he ate eggplant Parmesan, and that night he was too weak to raise his own body, which had slid too far down in the bed. My mom and I tried to hoist him by each grabbing an armpit, but we were fearful of hurting his now too thin limbs. I got up on the bed, straddled him and grabbed him around the torso. "Hold onto me," I instructed. We held each other in a tight embrace, as tight as his arms could muster, and I lifted his body up into position. Who thinks when we lift up our little babies, that one day they will be lifting us? We hugged a little longer.

In the kitchen my mom and I talked in a sad, hushed tone. How long can we physically do this? we wondered. Up until now it had taken no physical stamina, just time and care and pampering, of which we both had plenty. Up until that night, he had been weak but not unable, even sitting daily on the deck overlooking the lake. Now he was dying and we didn't know how long it would be.

Overnight, his decline continued at the same rapid pace. His breathing was labored and his eyes were heavy. We called those close-by. "Come

now," we told them, for now was all we had. And they came — his children
and some grandkids, his brother and nephews—and we waited. We sat and
held my dad's hands and rubbed his legs and wiped his face with cool cloths
and spoke through tears in low, calm voices.

All morning, everyone was in and out of the room, the house, and
with each entrance a new wave of grief washed over us. The little kids were
there too, earnestly in and out of the room with their play and myriad cousins.
Occasionally, they'd forget death was at hand, only to solemnly remember.
"Grandpa's dying," they'd announce in their serious, curious tone—half state-
ment/half question.

On the porch, the five-year-old picked up the baby from the playpen. We watched questioningly, as we would watch anyone removing a
contented baby from a playpen. The five-year-old turned, gestured toward
the baby with her head and informed, "She needs to see Grandpa." The big
sister carried the little sister in to sit with her dying grandfather whom she
would know only from stories. I imagined a future conversation in which she
would ask, "Did I know him?" and we would take out the picture of the two
of them together, her face cupped by his tender hand, and I would tell her
stories of the vibrant dad I had and the summer of his death.

The day went on, with food brought to the back door by neighbors
who knew and felt the vibe, or who had heard from one of us across the
fence. Some we left uninformed, unable to bring them in just yet, like the
woman across the street in her robe, smoking on her front porch, Do you
know someone's dying over here? I wondered. I stared a minute, then waved
and went back into the house.

Inside, the natural shifts of people continued as we held my dad
and rubbed his feet and fed him a crushed pain pill mixed with water. Like
feeding a baby bird, we put the syringe in the corner of his mouth and
dripped it in slowly. Thankfully, that was all his pain needed as he breathed
on heavily, rhythmically.

The little ones were in and out, peering through the screen door in
their wet bathing suits, intrigued, entranced by this life ending. Throughout
the morning they popped in randomly to check out the scene, feel the forces,

look at the faces and marvel at the fact that all these adults they knew and loved were all crying together. And when they caught our eye, our faces lifted through our tears and they marveled again that we could smile while we wept.

After lunch, an older grandchild came out to the kitchen, "Grandma, his breathing is changed all of a sudden." And indeed it had to a faster, shallower rhythm. Now we all came in together, including the kids, focused on the task of dying. We circled the bed and held my dad and each other, all linked around the room. My mom asked us all to release him, remove our hands from his body, stand silently, and let him go.

His breathing stopped and this silence was met by the exclamations of a three-year-old boy with his fingers in his ears and his face in the couch, beseechingly calling, "CAN YOU HEAR ME? CAN YOU HEAR ME"? My dad returned just for a second, maybe to say goodbye to a grandson that wouldn't remember. Then the stillness released him after all. His lifelong prayers for a happy, peaceful death were answered.

We cleaned him in a tender post-mortem bath, donned him in fresh white cotton, combed his hair and sat with him and with each other; grateful now for the uncle that told us not to panic at death but rather to linger in the passing. As we sat, the sky darkened from blue to steel gray and the clouds opened and it poured the kind of rain that makes conversations stop at the futility of not being heard. We all exalted and the kids ran out in it led by their fifteen-year-old cousin and together they all raced across the lawn and dove into the lake.

While the rain teemed down and my dad lay dead, we sat on the covered back porch to a meal sent over at the perfect time and a table magically prepared by someone, who knows, maybe us in our blind grief. A few hours later, we called and the funeral home picked him up. They admired the room in which he died; picture windows and glass door framing two different views of the water. They commented on the size of the crowd and at the kids in the room, and smiled appreciatively that this death was not lonely.

The five-year-old stayed and watched as they wrapped her grandfather in crisp white cotton sheets, leaving only his face showing. They then placed his shrouded body in the black bag, zipping it up to his chin, again leaving his face. They lifted him ever so gently and walked out to the hearse followed by the five-year old who perhaps never again would think of death as scary. The obituary read, "Dean Charles Noll passed away at home on August 3rd, 2003. His death was gentle. He is survived by the stories we tell."

Bernadette Noll is an author, copywriter, facilitator, and co-founder of Slow Family Living. From that website, we read, "It is our desire to help families and individuals find ways to slow things down, not with a recipe or a prescription, but rather by questioning how things are going, and finding ways that work for them. It is our biggest intention to help families find ways to slow things down, connect and enjoy life together." (http://slowfamilyliving.com/who-are-we/)

You can learn more about Bernadette's life and work at http://bernadettenoll.net/

Your Mom is so Sweet

Many of the stories I share are poignant and sweet. I don't mean to "sanitize" the end of life. It isn't always "precious." Not everyone has idyllic families. Not all have made peace with their past. Death and the dynamics around it are also messy and chaotic and imperfect and real, just like life. Most often, it's a mix of the positive and the challenging—and it ain't always pretty.

We seek to model treating patients with dignity, but we also owe the same dignity to their families. We should never assume that the person we're seeing today is the same version of the person whom the family has known for decades. On some level, we see their public face. We see a person often far softer than who they may have been for a lifetime to their family.

Even in the same family, members may have completely different relationships with each other, with some having more positive experiences, or recollections of those experiences, than others. My older brothers remember close bonds and happy times spent with my extended family. By the time I came along, those connections had changed significantly and, as the youngest, I have no memory of the stories they share.

We never know the whole story and must always remember this because it devalues the family and the relationships they sometimes have with one another to assume everyone had a good relationship with or were treated well by the patient. To gloss over this aspect of care honors no one and can harm many. We try hard to remember that when we speak with families. We don't always get it right. For instance, consider the following story:

The kind-hearted and well-intended hospice volunteer in front of me gushed, "Your mom is so SWEEEEET!" I cringed inwardly, and probably stopped breathing. The daughter couldn't really see me, as I was standing a bit behind her. We both stood facing this brand new and very eager part of my hospice team.

Over the daughter's shoulder, I tried to give a subtle shake of my head "No" to the volunteer, with a look that attempted to silently scream, "Please stop…that's not a good idea!" She didn't get it, and began saying a bit more about how wonderful the mother, a patient for whom we were caring, was and what a joy she was to visit.

I don't know if it was the stiffened back of the daughter, or my subtly sliding my finger across my neck in the some-what universal, "Cease and desist" signal that finally got her attention, but at last her gushing petered out into a few uncomfortably mumbled, "I'm-not-sure-exactly-what-I-did-but-I-know-I-just-stepped-in-it-big-time" words and she made a hasty exit.

I smiled as much reassurance as I could at the back-pedaling volunteer, and told her I would get with her before we both left the facility that afternoon to, "catch up" (so I could explain a little about the situation).

I don't blame her. Human interactions are tricky. Add the stress of illness and grief and it's really hard to navigate. Now try being a brand new volunteer, or even staff member, still getting all the necessary training and experience to develop the art of this whole hospice thing, and I can cut people plenty of slack!

In fact, I often say that volunteers are one of the most critical parts of our team, and I mean that, sincerely. "You guys are paid to come see us," one patient said to me. "We know you care, but when someone volunteers to come?! We know they really must care to do this with no paycheck attached."

Besides, volunteers have the time to take—the time to see and hear patients in ways we staff aren't always able. Nurses are focused on medications and symptoms; social workers must focus on logistics such as helping families navigate Medicaid and emotional dynamics; and chaplains are tending to spiritual distress. A volunteer will be more likely to ask what kind of magazines someone likes, and then bring it to them the next time they visit!

But when any of us in this industry misstep, the already raw patients and families feel it far more. After this unfortunate exchange, the daughter turned to face me, arms locked straight down by her side and fists and jaw clinched under ash-white skin, "I can't stand it when people do that. I mean, I get it, but geez it really hurts."

Again, accepting patients where they are and granting them dignity does not mean to whitewash the reality of who they are, how they've been, and what is the true circumstance of their relationships. We so often feel we cannot speak ill of the dead or dying but, even if your belief system says that the person will become a saint in the next life, if you believe in a life after this one, the dying person ain't there, yet! They get to have the dignity of being a full human being, which is to be imperfect, and at times, even a real pain in the butt, or worse, destructive.

When patients are dying and the family is standing around, not certain what to say or do, I'll often encourage them to process, if they're open to it, by asking "What are you going to miss when the time comes that the person dies?" We use the actual word—die...they will not "pass," (although flatulence can often occur when a body relaxes completely); they are not "lost" (so we will not be putting their faces on milk cartons). It's ok and even helpful to use the real words.

Most often, loved ones will share their stories and laugh and cry. At times, when the person has lived life the hard way, it can be a little more challenging to answer this one—and sometimes, a lot more challenging. For all of them, I wait until a natural lull in responses to that first question, and then ask, "Since they are/were human, and therefore imperfect, what are you not going to miss about them?"

This one gets a bit of a stunned reaction, as if they are waiting for either lightning or Miss Manners to come strike me for even suggesting such honesty. "Can we say that?" some will ask. "Can we say it in front of him? I mean, you guys say he likely can still hear us even though he's not responding…"

"I don't encourage anyone to be abusive, but he knows what he was like and, while he may have his own side of the story, nothing you say will likely be a surprise to him," I assure them.

Some answer immediately after I ask the question. Multiple times, several members of the family have answered in stereo with the same response.

Often, even the things that were challenging that won't be missed still have a tone of affection and laughter to them like stubbornness or lame jokes. "We never could get Dad to stop all his cussin'," one family said, "even around the grandkids! They just learned to ask before they used any of 'Poppa's words' because they knew they would get a spanking for saying a lot of them!"

But sometimes, there is no laughter about the imperfections, because the pain is too deep, too raw, too long-standing, and has yet to completely heal. Sometimes, the pain or disconnect is still on-going.

In the particular case of this story, the "sweet" mother had actually been, according to her daughters, an alcoholic without recovery, mean and abusive, most of their lives. She treated everyone else with the greatest kindness, but reserved her most venomous and hateful words for her children.

In the early days of caring for all of them, I sensed something was amuck. Then one day, I came up the hallway of the skilled nursing facility where she lived and was almost to the door of her room when I heard her voice speaking. It was clearly her voice, but in a tone and using words I had never heard from her before.

I stopped short, not certain what was going on and not wanting to barge in if it wasn't a good time. Then I heard one of her daughters speak, calmly, patiently, but wearily resigned.

The mother said some of the most hateful things to her daughter, the very child whom she raved about being such a, "wonderfully devoted and caring daughter;" whom she was, "lucky to have" on my weekly visits. She scolded her daughter for "dumping" her in the facility and "stealing" her money and having, "never been any good for anything in your whole life…"

I wasn't sure what to do. I took a half step forward, and could see the slumped-shouldered daughter standing at the foot of her mother's bed, futilely trying to arrange items on the shelf according to her mother's barked orders in a way that would finally make her happy. But there was clearly no pleasing her.

I stood for a moment, out of sight of the patient, but looking to the daughter. She saw me, glanced at her mother, and then made an excuse to leave the room for a moment to refill the bedside water pitcher. I'll not repeat the nasty rant thrown at the daughter's back as she walked out.

Once in the hallway, the daughter slumped with her back against the wall and leaned her head against it, eyes closed. Without moving she whispered, "So I guess you heard all that?"

"Enough" I said. "Would you like to talk about it?"

The story poured out. She talked about how difficult it was to care for her mother given her life-long, and on-going, treatment and yet her guilt if she did not care for her and the extra burden of the secret. No one in their extended family or friends had any clue how the woman could be. Honestly, had I not heard it, it might have been a little hard for me to wrap my head around. We talked about how this complicated her grief, how to set boundaries to protect and care for herself, and where she could go to get support for the long-standing trauma.

When we come into a situation, we know so little of the story. Even when we are told stories, we always trust that there's more we do not know. To insert ourselves into the triangle and decide that we know who is right or wrong, to make excuses or minimize, or to jump on the wagon and vilify serves no one. But we can validate persons' feelings. We can sympathize with their experience and how the situation is impacting them. None of that requires our, "taking sides" or treating anyone differently.

We are not there to do family therapy or "fix" decades-old patterns. We are there to provide support for the end of life. We can use the information that is shared to help us be more aware of how the grief process and medical care are being impacted by those patterns. Beyond that, we use the opportunity to invite people to access support—therapy, support groups, various 12-step recovery programs—and always in conjunction with the other members of the team, especially the social worker. We in hospice must know where our role ends and other professionals' tasks begin. We cannot be all things to all people.

But we can be mindful because we know that we do not know the whole story and we never want to perpetuate unintentional harm by assuming the Leave It to Beaver or Family Ties type of family closeness exits. So we do not pretend to know what it was like to be raised by a younger version of mom or dad.

When performing funerals for such circumstances, it's an honest challenge. How are we honest without disparaging one who is no longer here to defend himself or herself? How do we say wonderful things about someone who acted destructively without adding even more harm onto the real (or even imagined) victims?

I follow the family's lead, but tend to take this hopefully honest, mediating, and healing stance. Every circumstance is different, but I try to state something like, "We remember all that he was and still is to those whose lives he touched. We honor and give thanks for those qualities that were life-giving (naming them) and we also acknowledge that, being human and therefore imperfect, there were moments when he was not his best self."

I add that maybe, just maybe, in his oh-so-human moments that we were called to find our better selves in order to be more patient and loving and even challenged to remember those times when we were only too human, ourselves. I ask for healing of old wounds and room to find forgiveness for our own freedom's sake. That in laying the one who has died to rest, that old stories might also find a place to be laid down when the time is right.

So far, this type of approach seems to have brought at least some healing to those involved. For all ministers, I ask that we approach such moments with the greatest humility, sensitivity, openness, while praying our "arses" off that we do no more harm than has already been experienced.

My job at a funeral that has an element of challenge, as I see it, is to help bring some closure. I strive to work with the family to develop a ritual that will set a healthy tone for the process of moving forward into a new way of life, without the deceased physically present in it. Letting go and moving on, especially when harm has been experienced, can be challenging and complicated.

I once heard a vision of heaven as this—it is a great banquet table where all are seated. To our left is the person whom we've most harmed in this world. To our right is the person who has most harmed us. As grace received translates into grace extended, all around the table, then we will all know the freedom of forgiveness and peace.

While this is not a story I usually share at funerals, I keep that story in mind. I do so because it reminds me to assume neither the worst nor the best of others and that whatever stories I am told about another, or whatever stories I tell myself about them, that there is always more—to them, to me, and to the story between us.

It helps keep me grounded in greater compassion, which isn't a bad place for me to be, whatever the story.

Contemplation

My friend was struggling with trying to help her aging and ailing parents. We were having an early lunch as she picked my brain for ideas and support. I heard the same story I hear often from adult children:

Mom's slowing down, the doctor says it's time for hospice. Mom isn't ready, she wants to try home health instead, but won't call home health to schedule an assessment. Dad's also slowing down, we're all worried that he's going to wear himself out trying to take care of her; they both know they need to move to an assisted living facility, but are dragging their feet.

My friend then described their most recent adventure, "Mom called and said, 'I know we need to get ready to move, but I need to clear out the house first. Come help me get started with the master closet.' I was so impressed with her taking initiative and relieved to finally have some forward momentum. So I went over, and, under her direction, I pulled every single thing out of their huge walk-in closet.

"Things were on the bed, on the chairs, on the floor, laid out everywhere. Mom took one look at everything, turned to me and said, 'Oh, I'm not really ready to get rid of any of this stuff. Put it all back.' I thought I was going to lose it right then and there. It wasn't all the work, which did stink, but it was getting my hopes up that we were finally making some progress just to have those hopes dashed to smithereens, again. I can't take this!"

"I know it feels rotten, and even hopeless," I affirmed, "but believe it or not, this actually was progress for her!" And then I asked, "You know she's at the contemplative stage, right?"

Confused and exasperated, my friend stammered, "Yes…no…maybe…wait…what?!"

In the psychology of health and behavior change, there is a theory called: "Stages of Change," developed in the late 1970s by Carlo DiClemente & James Prochaska that provides a model for understanding how people go about making changes. (http://her.oxfordjournals.org/content/15/6/707.full) The second step is "contemplation," in which people know they need to make a change, and may even take some practice steps, but they're still on the fence and not really ready to commit to an action.

I asked my friend, "Have you ever known you needed to break up with someone, but you weren't quite yet ready to do it? So you do a trial break-up and then reconcile before the big finale? That's contemplation, you know it probably needs to be done, but you need to sit with that knowledge for a while, try it on, see how it feels, and get used to the idea of moving forward.

"While a pain in the rear for you, your mom was experimenting with the idea. She got as close as she could, played around with how it felt to let go of her things and her house, and then back-pedaled quickly. It may feel like regression, but it's actually a good sign that she's getting herself ready to make this move."

My friend's face relaxed, her shoulders dropped down from where they had been hanging out around her earlobes, and she let out a relieved sigh. "Just hearing that makes me feel so much better. And it makes a lot of sense. I think I can let this go, now."

We had talked for weeks about my typical counsel for adult children regarding changes that they feel must be made, but their parents are resisting: Give them space. Speak your feelings or concerns once, but after that, it's nagging and will only push them to entrench in their viewpoint even further and resist the idea and even you.

So long as they are not a danger to themselves or others, they have the right to make their own decisions, and there is even a saying in the healthcare industry that people, "have the right to fall."

When a patient is determined to walk while living in a skilled nursing facility, for instance, and they either forget or refuse to use their walker or wheelchair, the staff is not allowed to restrain them in any way, not with "seatbelts" or medications or anything that inhibits their free motion. To do so is a violation of their rights, and the state agencies that monitor the care of seniors are highly sensitive to protecting those rights.

Staff must show that all reasonable measures have been taken to assure their safety, but ultimately a sentient human being has the right to walk even if it is certain that they will fall. It is a matter of dignity and free will and protection against abuse. Many adult children feel guilty if they do not "force" their parents to do or not do something, fearing that if they get hurt then they will feel awful and/or others will judge them as not taking good care of mom or dad. It's a frustrating and scary and painful spot to be in.

Not only is it their right, it also is sometimes the best way to guarantee their willingness to finally try something different. Often we humans need to try, "just one more time," or 10 or 20, just to make sure we really can't do something. If we're stopped before then, we'll always wonder, "what if," and we'll struggle to adapt to the change, blaming others for imposing it on us.

But sometimes, if we're allowed to suffer the consequences of our actions, it can be exactly the motivation we need to be willing to finally try something different.

Before I get myself into legal trouble, let me be clear that every situation is different, so I encourage you to consult with your family, your physicians, and other providers, social workers, family legal counsel, etc. and make the decision that is most appropriate for your unique situation. I'm only speaking generally of the human need to try and push until life, not another human, pushes back.

Letting go of control when we feel ultimately responsible is challenging, but sometimes, dropping the rope and resigning from the tug of war is exactly the shift in energy that is needed to bring real change to a situation. Sometimes, the tug of war itself can be used as a distraction to take attention away from the real issue.

The bottom line is that sometimes the most responsible, loving, efficient, and sane thing we can do is let another person have their process. We can set boundaries if their process is making us insane, and we do not have to agree to enable behavior with which we do not agree. Finally, we can accept the ultimate boundary that their life is their own, and they deserve to find their way, knowing that when we intervene, sometimes we stand in the way of exactly the path that will be of greatest value to them. We can disengage to stay sane, trust them to find their way, and walk with them with a lot less anxiety, guilt, and frustration, and just enjoy being their daughter, son, loved one, rather than trying to play a role that isn't ours to play.

There's a Sweet Spirit

I received the call that she was dying. I waved as I rushed past the nurses' station at the acute care in-patient facility, letting them know I had arrived. She had been at the facility the last few days for symptom management. I walked into her room, apparently moments after her last breath. The family hadn't even let the nurses know, yet, so they could "officially" pronounce her death. They were just taking their time saying their goodbyes. They invited me to stay.

She and her husband had been high-school sweethearts. He, like his wife, was in his early sixties. Their grown children were in the room, along with a few other close relatives and life-long friends. They shared stories about her.

I did what I often do to try to help families walk through that moment of letting go. I asked what they were and weren't going to miss about her. They talked and laughed and cried as they shared. Finally, I asked if they knew what she believed came next for her, if anything, once she stepped from this life into the next. They shared their beliefs and hopes for her to be at peace and with those she loved.

I stood with the family around her in her bed, holding hands, and said a prayer, appropriate for their views and needs.

I said my goodbyes as I went, with their permission, to get the nurse to "pronounce" her death. My hand was on the door handle and the heavy wood was already a few inches open before I felt this tap, tap, tap on my shoulder.

No one was behind or beside me. But I was clear there was something more I was supposed to say.

In a moment of "holy tremble" (those times when I feel a prompting to do or say something, but am not completely sure what it is), I cautiously pushed the door those few inches back into its latch, and turned again into the room. What I said came from that place of silence and stillness inside me; with words coming out that I hear for the first time only once they've left my own lips: "You know, as chaplains, we get pretty good at reading the energy in a room when we come into it, whether folks are charged and angry or struggling with despair, and I have to say, (looking to the husband), you and your wife did something really "right." There's a sweet spirit in this room. Can you feel it?"

You could have heard the proverbial pin drop as their jaws all hit the floor. I knew I had stumbled onto something. I wasn't sure what, so I just waited, hoping it was nothing detrimental to the family, but trusting guidance and life to unfold as it needed.

The eldest daughter finally asked me, "Did you stop and talk to the nurses on your way in?"

"No," I responded, "I knew she was close to death, so I came right in. Why?"

"Yesterday, Mom 'rallied,'" the daughter said. "She sat on the back porch (of the facility) and ate a Big Mac and drank a Diet Coke and told stories and cracked jokes with everyone. As night came, she was completely worn out. When she lay down in bed for the night, we all knew it was very likely the last time we would ever talk with her.

"She drew us all close to the bed, because she was so tired she could barely speak above a whisper, and she said, 'There's a sweet spirit in this room. Can you feel it?' I remember it so vividly because it struck me as odd. You see, Mom was a lot of things, but 'sweet' just wasn't one of them!"

The rest of the family and friends laughed softly and nodded in agreement.

"It's just not how she would have ever described herself and certainly not how she would have ever spoken," said the daughter. "So I want to know, how in the world you knew to say that?!"

All I could do was smile softly in slightly stunned amazement and ask, "What do you think?"

Looking around the room at her loved ones, the daughter replied, "I think Mom stopped you on your way out the door and asked you to give us one more message that it's all okay."

Even the most faithfully religious people, if they feel they are in safe space to say so, will admit to having days, or decades, of doubt…agnosticism at the least, and even heavy doses of atheism. I certainly am not immune to that.

But day after day, things beyond my ability to explain or comprehend happen around us in this work that humble me, give me pause, and assure me that something greater than me is working in this world. I know I can trust it to hold us all and help us find our way, if only we can listen and let it be present with us.

Here's the best part—I no longer need to know what it is. I no longer have to understand it. Call it a Greater Consciousness, call it G-d, call it Chance, I honestly do not need it to even have a name. I just know that it brings me peace.

At one point in my upbringing, I was taught not to question G-d or faith because it was a sign of weakness. Then I was adopted into a faith tradition that encouraged thought and questioning. Now I am free to ask and question and doubt not as an abandonment of faith, but because my faith is strong enough to handle it.

Increasingly, I'm calmly comfortable when I don't "know" the answers, and I angst less and feel abandoned less often when the answer isn't clear. This is not because I've been told, "to just trust G-d and accept the mystery," but because I experience and live in the face of that mystery every day, and even at times wrestle with it.

But always, always the mystery holds me and unfolds in time to reveal beauty and wholeness out of the broken places, and shows me the goodness that can come from tragedy. I see gifts that can come not because of, but in spite of, that which I perceive in the moment to be "bad."

And with such awe-inspiring experience behind me, that is now one thing that I can never, ever doubt.

Little Boy Lost

I'm a little boy, lost and alone in the woods. I do not know where to turn or where there is anything or anyone to guide me.

His hair was stark white, more than a little reminiscent of Einstein. It was unusually long and unkempt compared to the military photos displayed proudly along the walls of the hallway we slowly moved past, as we ambled from his living room to his front porch. The once-imposing 6'3" frame shook with Parkinson's and a lack of muscle tone appeared to remove several inches from his height as he stooped over his walker. The Parkinson's also sought to end his independence. My hospice group had been called in to help ease his challenges.

He spoke in a gentle, precise, and formal voice. He shared with me his pride at the appointed position as a reader of sacred texts during services in his faith community. It did not escape me that he once commanded legions as well as the spoken word, but his control was now slowly dissipating

We sat in lawn chairs on the brick and concrete rectangle that faced the street and enjoyed the sun, and the purple popsicles he insisted on sharing with me. He became unusually quiet on this visit. Ordinarily, week after week, he peppered me with theological questions and attempted to debate various ideologies, philosophies, and doctrines. I would gently deflect sharing my beliefs and remind him that was not why I was there—but not today. Today, he was unusually quiet.

He paused with a deep breath to compose the tremor that shook his voice, brought on by emotion, neurology, or perhaps both. He looked down at the purple puddle gradually forming between his feet on the concrete.

That shift gave gravity the chance to finally pull the tears rimming the lids of his cerulean blue eyes over their edges. He didn't bother to hide or wipe them from his cheeks as he finally looked up at me and said,

"I am like a little boy, lost and alone in the woods.
I do not know where to turn
or where there is anything or anyone
to guide me,
and I am afraid…"

Minutes passed as he turned and faced the fields in the distance. Then, with a lift of his chin and slight tilt and turn of his head, he cut his proud and misty eyes toward their corners to look back at me. The nearest bushy white eyebrow was now sardonically aloft; he continued,

"…but I suppose that is why you are here."

We sat in silence as the sun and our tongues continued to melt the treats. Finally, I asked him about being lost in the unknown, about his relationship with mystery, and the challenge of finding space to sit with both until more is revealed. I unfolded and handed him a well-worn and creased page from my hip pocket, then spoke the words from memory:

I dwell in the mystery of the great unknown
Fluid, beautiful, and free.
I dance with the wind and relish each breath
Ecstatic each day just to be.
I sing with the joy of the planets and stars,
I laugh with the waves and the sea,
For I am the spirit forever unfolding
Unbounded, eternal, and free

(Donna Miesbach www.donnamiesbach.com)

"What do you think?" I asked. He turned the paper over, then once again, and traced the fuzzy edges and folded lines with his finger, staring quietly at the words. Finally, he smiled a bit sheepishly, "The part of me that likes to know, that has long loved the established nature and certainty of code, honor, liturgy, and creed…absolutely HATES it." Then, with an exhale of peaceful resignation, like the sigh that comes when we lie back into our favorite chair after a long day of work and surrender ourselves to rest, he said, "But I suppose it would be nice to not need 'to know' for once. Maybe that's the final lesson this old colonel gets to learn."

At his request, I prayed for his peace as he sought to feel the invisible presence of that which he believed held and carried him in the midst of those lonely and frightening woods until he found his way—or his way found him. It was humbling for this proud and distinguished man to admit his struggles and pain. It was challenging to make room inside myself to sit with him as he wrestled, in slow silence. I had to quell my need to fill the space with questions. I got to consider his words quietly and walk beside him without needing to "fix" his pain or believe that I knew how to direct his journey. I just needed to simply be present with it—with him, and trust him to find his way.

An offering of words here, an invitation there, but ultimately the path through the landscape was his and his alone. The good news? He didn't have to be alone as he found his way. And I was not alone, as I joined him. As it turns out, the mystery of the great unknown, which can seem so overwhelming, isn't nearly as scary when we face it together.

Moaning to Singing

She was a young woman who had both loved and suffered much in her short life. She came from a close, religiously devout family who remained at her side. A fever in her teens left her forever changed. As a result, she was challenged by both mental illness and physical limitations. Her extended family, including nieces and nephews, loved her for her exuberant love and fullness of life, which included singing, jokes, and laughter.

When I met her, she was in her early thirties and could still speak just enough to articulate that she did not know why G-d wouldn't let her die. Her faith was strong, but she questioned why she was "Still here, and not in heaven with my baby boy" (her only child had died shortly after birth). As her body deteriorated and seizures from her condition debilitated her, her greatest suffering was the spiritual pain of feeling betrayed and abandoned by a G-d who would, in her view, allow her to "Suffer this way and not take me home."

I did not claim to have any answers for her. I did not pretend to understand. I wanted to. It was hard to see her so distraught. But again, my job is not to "fix" the pain I witness. I do not tell others how to believe. Instead, I am called to walk with persons as they wrestle with their own faith, their own questions, and find their own answers.

It was not my place to pretend to know how she could best resolve her struggle. It was not for me to know how her journey "should" unfold. It was not for me to rob her of the dignity of finding her own answers. As the quote from Lao Tzu in the *Introduction* has taught me, if I do not trust them to find their own way on their journey, they will not trust me. And, I may also mistakenly teach them to not trust themselves, or even G-d, if I put myself into the position of: "The one who has all the answers."

I turned to the language and theology of her own faith, (as she and her family had described it to me) and responded to her questions with, "I don't know how or when your prayers to die will be answered, but I do trust that until that time comes, G-d's angels will be singing and watching over you and will carry you home when the time is right."

Without missing a beat, she retorted, "Well tell them angels to shove over and make some room, because I want to come home NOW!"

I had failed her. I tried to put a Band-Aid on her pain rather than sit with her in it. As a seminary professor of mine once said, "Remember, Job's friends got it right, until they opened their damn mouths".

In the Judeo-Christian scriptures, Job lost everything and was suffering. At first, Job's friends came and sat with him silently for days (in sackcloth and ashes) in the Jewish tradition of mourning called, "Shiva." But after a period of time, they were no longer able to sit with the mystery of Job's suffering (the same trap I fell into). They each began to take turns, spewing a different monologue about why Job was suffering.

It was, to many scholars' thinking, the writer's way of wrestling with the question of "theodicy" (why a good G-d "permits" evil) and sorting through the prevailing theories of the "whys" of suffering, which included blaming Job for sinning and causing G-d's wrath.

G-d finally speaks to Job from within the middle of a storm. For me, it is not what G-d says, but the fact that G-d simply was there with Job that matters. G-d entered the struggle and was present with him and his suffering as Job wrestled with his own questions.

My professor's words rang in my ears as I realized that I would do well to do more sitting with other's pain and being present with them as they wrestled with it, rather than open my mouth and believe I have something important to say.

And so, to her demands that the angels, "shove over and make some room…," I simply responded, "I hear you. I wish that for you, too" and continued to stroke her fevered brow with a cool cloth.

As our visits continued over the weeks, she quickly became unable to speak coherently, and so I would sing to her the hymns I knew she loved from our previous times together. Other times, I would just sit with her in silence, until it came time to leave, and I would pray aloud for peace and the presence of G-d as she waited for answers to her struggles and questions.

When she could not speak, I said aloud for her, "G-d, we don't understand why this is happening, why death and the freedom that comes with it are so slow to come. And so we wait, and ask for your hand to hold this space and give her peace until the answers do come, one way or the other."

The last time I saw her she was moaning quietly, as she so often did at those times when I entered her room. I pulled up a chair and sat beside her hospital bed. Words of comfort and reassurance did nothing. And again, I realized I was trying to fix it and make it better for her. When will I learn? I thought. Medicines had already been given, but physical signs seemed to again indicate that her suffering was more spiritual than physical. And so I joined her the only way I knew how. I entered into her moaning with her.

Often, when a patient is physically hurting or is anxious and their breathing is erratic, I'll enter their breathing with them, matching their rhythm and pace and then slowly shift mine to be calmer and deeper. Quite often, they will join me until we are both breathing more peacefully.

So this day, I moaned with her. I attempted to sit with her in sackcloth and ashes and not fix it, but just be with her in it. And as we moaned, me matching my moaning to her timbre and rhythms, her groans began to lessen and soften. It was almost as if she felt heard and affirmed, and I would like to believe that it took a bit of the edge off her pain.

We continued moaning, but slowly I turned my sounds to humming. I hummed her rhythm and pitch, and then she joined me in doing the same. I then shifted to pick up the tune of some of those favorite hymns we had sung together previously, and again, she joined me. So we hummed hymn after hymn until her sounds softened, then ceased, and her breathing evened out to a more calm rhythm. I then turned my humming to singing softly over her.

A couple of days later, the angels moved over and made room for her to join them.

Perhaps I was still trying to fix it, make it better. That is, after all, why so many of us feel called to this work, to help people find peace and comfort in the spiritual realm. The difference was that I wasn't dismissing her pain anymore; I wasn't covering it over, denying it, or ignoring it with platitudes and clichés.

I just heard her pain and joined her in it. Once I did, she then joined me, and we walked together to her place of comfort.

World-renowned psychiatrist, Herbert Adler, wrote in the *Journal of General Internal Medicine* (Nov. 2002, 17 (11) 883-90 doi: 10.1046/j.1525-1497.2002.10640.x) that therapeutic listening can be thought of as analogous to "hemodialysis" in which the patient speaks "anguish born of fear, isolation, and helplessness" and a good listener circulates back to the patient these fears processed through by the listener's "compassionate equanimity." In short, as one nurse told me not long ago, "We shut up and show up."

Equanimity is defined (dictionary.reference.com) as: "mental calmness, composure, and evenness of temper, especially in a difficult situation." I can only sit with "compassionate equanimity" in the midst of another's pain if I can find enough calm within myself to do so. I can only be present with them if I can be present within myself.

It takes courage to sit in silence with ourselves. Facing the darkness of the unknown is almost impossible without the ability to do so. As scary as sitting with only our own company can be, we can trust that something greater than us will find us there in the midst of the abyss and help us find our way out again. We will not get lost there forever. When we face our fears and learn to face ourselves, without the distractions of music, television, others, and even our own incessant internal chatter, we can come to know ourselves well. Out of that ability to be with ourselves, we increase our ability to be with others without needing to fill the space.

Over the millennia, countless others have taken the inward journey and survived to tell the tale. And if we want to deepen in our capacity to sit with others' pain, we must first learn to sit with "compassionate equanimity" with our own.

The Shaman

He didn't want a chaplain. A couple had gone and tried to visit him, but he just wasn't interested. Then one day I received a call from his social worker. The patient wanted me to call. I did.

He said he wanted a Shaman to come visit him because he had spiritual questions and Native spirituality was the closest fit for his beliefs. He was surprised that not only did I not balk at the request, but I actually knew some local Shamanic practitioners to call.

As I tried via phone to coordinate a visit for him, he talked. He ranted. He griped. For weeks, and weeks, he canceled and rescheduled and hemmed and hawed. He could not commit to a time for a Shaman to come visit. But he would spend another 30 minutes on the phone with me sharing his complaints. He blasted Christianity—its hypocrisy and history of violence and arrogance.

He was surprised when, instead of arguing or defending religion, I actually affirmed his feelings. "Across time and space, humans have misused religion and done awful things in the name of G-d, and some followers of Christianity have been amongst the worst offenders," I shared.

There was a long pause on the other end of the phone line—so long that I checked to see if we had been disconnected. I finally heard a softened and somewhat perplexed voice saying, "I think maybe you can come out and visit me."

I did.

He greeted me in jeans, barefoot and bare-chested. A long silvered black braid flowed down his back. Tattoos, some apparently prison-issue, covered most of his upper body. He was emaciated to the point of being almost skeletal, and had a haunted look in his eyes and face that spoke of something else.

He had a cigarette in one hand and the stained convenience-store-issued tumbler, which I learned he always carried, in the other. It was filled with half high-protein shake and half vodka. It was 10:00 a.m.

As we visited in his apartment, he told me of his childhood, family, his loves, his children. He showed me treasures from the refurbishing projects he loved to fiddle with and which items in his house he wanted to go to which loved one. He told me of his faith journey from devout Catholicism to disillusionment with organized religion; his wandering through Buddhism in his time abroad in the service, to his current Native beliefs, and everything else in between.

Week by week, he talked, he smoked, he ranted, he seemed to dance around his real pain, and I gave witness. Then one day he volunteered his "confession." He believed he was not worthy of being forgiven and feared what was coming after death.

I asked him about his beliefs regarding forgiveness in Native Spirituality. We dialogued back and forth for hours over the weeks, mostly with him asking me questions, which I deferred back to his own wisdom and experience. He told me of his nightmares and dreams and considered what they meant. But still, he couldn't get past thinking that grace and forgiveness were for everyone else, just not him. He anguished.

Finally, I asked him why he had originally wanted a Shaman, and if he wanted one now. He said he thought he was beyond help, but he had hoped that a ritual would help him find freedom from the guilt and fear he just couldn't get past. I asked him what that ritual would look like? How it would feel? What it would hopefully accomplish? And the ritual evolved.

Finally, months after those first phone calls, he put out his cigarette, drained the last of his tumbler's vodka/protein shake mixture, and sat cross-legged, barefoot, bare-chested, and with the talisman of multiple faiths hanging around his neck from a crucifix to a sterling silver eagle's feather. He sat on the faded blue shag carpet in the middle of his apartment as I walked around him with a bundle of dried sage and lavender to perform a smudging, baptizing him in the smoke believed to be cleansing in Native spirituality. Throughout the ritual, I read Catholic and Buddhist and Native prayers.

As I doused the bundled sage, I closed with the "Our Father" from the Catholic tradition, placed my hands on his head, and spoke to him words of reassurance of G-d's pardon, asking G-d's blessings upon him. It was silent for a long time. I finally removed my hands from his head and sat on the floor across from him.

When he opened his eyes, something had shifted. Though still gaunt and wasted physically from illness, the "haunted" look was gone. He sat quietly for a long time—I had never heard him actually be quiet even half that long in all the months I had known him combined! Finally, he looked up at me and slowly gave a few small nods of his head, as if to say, "It's done."

He was a lot quieter every visit after that. No more rants against religion. No more attempts at theological debate. No more dancing around issues and no more angst-filled doubts. Instead, he spoke more of the legacy he wanted to leave behind to his family, especially his children, wanting them to know how much he loved them. He called and reconciled with family members. He smoked, he drank his Vodka shake, but something was different. He said he couldn't describe it, but he felt "free," and he certainly looked that way. "It's like it's all okay now, in some way," he said.

I didn't ask for an explanation. According to the *Book of Sacrament* by Tad W. Guzie (pg.39), ritual is: "an outward and visible sign of an inward and invisible act of grace." I had no need to try to capture it in words. The impact was too tangible in him to need more description. A few weeks later, he died.

Had I not been able to hold space with his anger and pain, had I not been open to whatever journey and mixture of ritual he needed to find his peace, I would have missed so very much. I would have failed him as his chaplain. Had I cringed at his venting or even once defended myself, my faith, or religion in general, I would have lost my chance to walk with him in the way that he needed. I'm thankful that did not happen because I would have missed out on one heck of a quest, with one heck of a man.

Ritual

She had been a professor and taught overseas for much of her adult life. She was intelligent and witty, with pale blue eyes that cast brilliantly against her backdrop of flowing white hair. But she was very quiet and reserved, so for a long time I wasn't certain how "clear" and lucid she was.

Dementia was amongst her co-morbidities (multiple diagnoses), and the staff at the skilled nursing facility where she resided stated she refused to go into the dining room because she said she could, "hear what everyone was thinking" and it was, "too loud" in her head when she went in there. As a result, many wrote her off as "senile." But I later learned those beautiful eyes missed little of what went on.

It took months. I would visit and carry on as much conversation as I could with little response from her. When I would try to slowly gather assessment information about her spiritual or religious background, she said little and declined to answer most of my questions. Again, I wasn't sure whether she did not know or did not want to say.

Given her hesitation, and not knowing what her beliefs were, I did not offer to pray, but said before I left each time, "If there is ever anything I can do to be of spiritual support, please let me know." I sensed treading lightly was the best approach. Each time I left and asked if she would like me to visit again, she said, "Oh yes, anytime."

The nurse indicated she discussed enjoying my visits, so I kept going back and persisted with the challenge of having a largely one-sided conversation. Slowly, she began to talk a bit with each visit.

Then one day she said, "I keep waiting for you to talk about religion to me."

"Is that something you'd like to discuss?" I asked.

"Not really" she said, "I tend to think that's private and don't like to discuss it."

"Then we don't have to. We can discuss whatever brings you peace and happiness."

She looked skeptical, but kept inviting me back. More months passed. She mentioned loving chewing gum because it helped keep her mouth from drying out during the day. With her nurse's permission, I stopped and got her a few variety packs on my way to the next visit.

You would have thought she was five years old and it was her birthday party, the way she went on and on about the gum. The look on her face was one of sheer delight and amazement.

That day, she mentioned being raised in a conservative Protestant denomination. I sat quietly to leave space for her to say more. When she did not, I finally asked what that had been like for her. She said a bit about it being, "okay, I guess, but that didn't last." I just said, "Oh?" She said no more. By now, I had learned the moments when there was a clear but non-verbal "No-trespassing" sign up around her, so I pushed no further.

Then one day, she was quite talkative, and asked me more about what exactly it was that I did for my hospice agency. "I work as a chaplain to people of all faiths, and people of no faith. I visit and do whatever I can to use their beliefs to help them access what brings them meaning and comfort."

She just stared at me for a long time. I sat in silence.

A couple of visits later, she said she thought it was good that I was so open, "because a lot of people have been hurt, like me." She didn't explain further, so I asked when this happened. "Oh, in my middle age, I guess. It happened slowly. I just felt more and more uncomfortable with it all. And finally, I could just never go back."

I asked if she found community somewhere else, and she said, "Not really, 'cause now I practice Wicca, and there aren't many communities in this area."

"Oh yeah," I said, "we just celebrated Beltane" (a Gaelic May Day festival celebrated still by Celtic neo-pagans and Wiccans).

"What? How do you know about Beltane?" she asked, seeming quite confused.

"Well, I have friends who are both Native American Pagan and Celtic Pagan, and they've taught me. Besides, as a chaplain to persons of all faiths, I try to understand as much as I can so I can be of service to all."

I asked if there were any rituals she missed from Wicca that I could bring to her in the skilled nursing facility.

"No," she said, "everything here is ritual."

Confused, I asked her to tell me more.

"Just listen," she said. I caught a glimpse of the teacher in her as her eyes shown, a slight smile on her lips, watching me, her newest pupil, to see if I would grasp the lesson.

As we sat in silence, I heard the obnoxious beep of an unanswered call light going off a few doors down. I've long said I could never work in a nursing facility because those beeps and buzzes would drive me bonkers, like fingernails on a chalkboard.

But then, I began to slowly hear other things—the wheels of a medicine cart rolling from room to room; the squeaking of a nurse's shoes as she went from a neighboring room back to the nurses' station; the whir of the floor waxer swooshing from side to side on the tiles outside her door, pushed by the maintenance man; the not-so-soft pattern of snores from her roommate in the next bed. There was a rhythm to the sounds as they wove themselves together into a blended song of, well, Life.

As I began to hear it, a smile of understanding rose on my face. My teacher beamed at me. "Medications come at the same time. The coming and going of residents to meals happens like clockwork. Aids and maintenance staff and family and friends all come and go in a fairly predictable pattern. It's all ritual. You just get to be with it until you sense it. And then, it's comforting, at least to me, just as any other ritual can be. So you see, Chaplain, I have all the ritual I need."

She went on to explain that she had always been "the sensitive sort" and picked up easily on the emotions of those around her. "Being in that dining room, with so many feelings: sadness, frustration, confusion…I sense all of it and it's simply too much. So I participate from my little island, here (indicating her bed), and notice what I can take in, as an Observer, witnessing it while so many rush past it."

I was the one with the badge, the religious degree, the ordination and title. But that day, like most days when I can really listen, I was also the student, learning from a source of wisdom far greater than me. When I cannot, or forget to sit and be with such spaces, what gifts I deny myself! When I can, the care I seek to bring is far more effective and I learn so much more.

Assuming Mary

I'd been told she was Catholic. The face sheet in her chart had the word in big block letters under "Religious Preference." I had not been able to reach her family by phone before I was required to visit and had only been able to leave a voicemail message for her daughter. (Per Medicare regulations, a patient must be assessed by each discipline within five days of admission.)

I prefer to have as much information as possible; especially when a patient is largely non-responsive, as I was told this patient was when she was admitted to hospice services. Family, friends, and facility staff are the best sources of information. I depend on them to tell me as clearly as possible what does and does not provide them spiritual comfort. I never want to assume, and I especially never want to be disrespectful of their beliefs.

I interviewed staff about what they knew about her and what appeared to them to give her the most peace. Those who provide daily care can become like a second family to a patient, and often know the nuances of their personalities and needs quite well.

As I walked into her room, the bulletin board over her bed had a prayer card from the Virgin of Guadalupe and a plastic rosary hanging from it. Her eyes were closed. Her frame was slight and she was curled almost into a fetal position.

I sat with her and talked about the pictures in her room that appeared to be of her family and pets. I held her hand gently (arthritis can make firm touch painful, so I try to be mindful of this) and talked to her, offering her a caring presence. I talked about the weather and described what I saw going on outside her window—a man mowing the lawn, a bird flitting to her windowsill, the leaves of the huge oak tree rustling in the hot Texas wind.

Before I left, I said the "Our Father," the Catholic version of what Protestants call "The Lord's Prayer," and was pleasantly surprised when she appeared to rouse a bit, eyes still closed, and mouthed most of the words to whisper the prayer with me.

As I was pulling my car out of the parking lot after my visit, her daughter returned my call. I was grateful to be able to share with her that her mother had responded enough to say the prayer.

There was a long silence on the other end of the line. Then, her daughter said, "Wow, that is amazing…especially considering that my mother is Jewish!"

Horrified, I fell all over myself apologizing. I don't believe I've ever groveled so much in my life, telling her I would never, ever have intentionally imposed any other religion on her mother or in any way disrespect her mother's faith. I told her about the face sheet, the prayer card, the rosary…"I am so very, very sorry. Please, please forgive me!"

"That's okay," the daughter laughed, "I just want to know where the hell she learned it?"

We later learned that a well-meaning group of Eucharistic ministers from a nearby Catholic church had left the prayer card and rosary on the patient's bulletin board when they were there to visit the Catholic patients who lived at the facility. The staff, seeing it and assuming this meant she was Catholic, put this on her face sheet. Our hospice staff saw the fact sheet and decorations in her room, and assumed the same. And then I joined the assumptions.

Apparently, the family accepted my groveling because when the time came that the patient died and I went to pay my respects, the family graciously invited me to sit Shiva with them.

Oh, the humbling, and thankfully gracious, ways our teachers show themselves.

Asking the Questions

If only I could throw away the urge to trace my patterns in your heart, I could really see you.

—**David Brandon,** *Zen in the Art of Helping*

One of the first lessons always taught regarding working with persons of other cultures and belief systems is to not assume what it means when they tell us they are _____ (fill in the blank). Labels may provide a general understanding of another and help bring order to a messy world, but they are not all defining. What being Pilipino and Catholic means to one person will vary amongst others who happen to be Pilipino and Catholic. Therefore, it's best to ask and not just assume.

Her chart said she was Christian Scientist. She had just been transferred to the skilled nursing facility after being hospitalized from a heart attack. As I walked down the hall toward her room to meet her for the first time, I spoke briefly with her son. He shared that his mother had been the leader responsible for starting the local Christian Science Reading Room in that city and spoke of her deep faith.

We entered the room and saw immediately that something was wrong. Voices were raised, the whir of an electronic blood pressure cuff was beginning, and the loud and rapid wheezing of the woman sounded incredibly strained. She had gone into severe respiratory distress and the paramedics who had transported her from the hospital were responding to her crisis.

I knew our hospice nurse was just down the hall, talking with the facility's charge nurse, sharing reports based on information they each had from the hospital, doctor, and family. I alerted them both that the patient was having trouble and rushed with them back down the hall to the room.

As a "good chaplain," I was trying to advocate for the patient. I extolled them that if she was resistant to interventions, out of respect for her faith, they should be mindful about not pushing her. It was my understanding that the founder of Christian Science taught that illness is an illusion and is best treated by prayer. While adherents are not required to eschew medical intervention, the church does uphold the belief that prayer is most effective if not combined with modern medicine.

Our nurse case manager and the charge nurse rushed into the room with me right beside them. I was still in the process of cautioning them to tread lightly when over my shoulder from the corner of the room I heard the patient ask, between her labored gasps, for a medicated breathing treatment and an anti-anxiety pill.

I stopped mid-sentence and whipped my head around toward her. The son, now standing beside his mother attentively, must have read the highly confused "WHAT?!" on my face. He laughed almost apologetically and reassured me by saying, "Oh, yeah…Mom has no problem with Western medicine."

Like Mighty Mouse: Here I come to save the day!, I was trying to honor her faith and help protect her from medical staff that might pressure her. I had made an assumption based upon what I thought I knew. Admittedly, there wasn't a lot of time in the midst of the breathing crisis to do a full assessment, but I had allowed myself to fill that void by making an assumption. The situation, while not dire, still reminded me to never assume that even the most faithful adherents of a particular belief system practice their faith in a prescribed, particular way.

Always ask. Always clarify. Always let them tell us what their faith means to them and what it is they need. This is a good lesson for medical staff, but I find it's most beneficial for me simply as a human being on the planet interacting with others, both strangers and those close to me.

Again, we like to think that we know, but until we ask, we can never be certain. Have the conversations with your loved ones now. What do they believe? What do they want and need? There are tools available, such as "Go Wish" cards (available at www.gowish.org) that can facilitate the conversation about what we want for ourselves at the end of our life. The more we can communicate, the greater the chance everyone involved will have a positive experience, which is always our goal.

Redemption

The idea of following patients on their journey and not imposing our own views on them can sometimes be more challenging than expected. At one time, I had two patients who believed G-d was punishing them by giving them their illness.

For one of them, the man from "The Shaman" story shared previously, the idea kept him feeling scared, ashamed, angry, and disconnected from G-d. Since this belief caused him great distress, we discussed alternatives that still fit his belief system to help him find peace.

For my other patient, however, the idea that G-d was punishing her was actually helpful to her! This confused me at first, until she explained that she had engaged in multiple affairs in her younger years. She believed her illness, an aggressive form of uterine cancer, was G-d's way of "cleansing" her of her "sin" in this life so she would not have to "pay for it on the Day of Judgment" in the next. She believed this illness was redemptive and was G-d's way of helping her get into heaven.

This was a new concept for me, and I'll be honest, I was taken aback. I'm reticent to share my theology with patients, and rarely do, as I do not want to sway their beliefs in any way whether overtly or even by subtle implication. It's an impossible standard to keep, as what we believe so easily slips into all that we say, but it is a crucial boundary to seek. Besides, I don't want to erect a barrier between myself and patients if my beliefs differ from theirs. I don't want to keep them from being open with me.

I could not tell her that her belief that G-d punishes is an anathema to my sensibilities. I could not share with her that to attribute such a characteristic to G-d in any way is a trigger for me. While this belief does not work for me, I had to acknowledge that it was working for her. It was actually bringing her comfort, healing, and peace so I had absolutely no business touching it!

I needed to watch to make certain that my triggers did not interfere with her process. I stayed in close contact with my colleagues and spiritual director to be mindful of how I was feeling and thinking under the surface. I intentionally found ways to affirm what was actually helpful and healing for her, emotionally and spiritually, without lying to her and claiming that I agreed with her.

I told her, "I'm so glad G-d is showing up for you this way, and being so good to you," and, "I'm grateful you're finding so much healing and comfort from this." Those things were true. I didn't need to share anything else with her but that.

She had peace, and my job was to affirm her peace. My true work became sitting with my discomfort so as to not in any way risk taking that peace away from her.

Sit with Me First

"Sit with me, first, then I'll let you walk with me."

I don't remember where I first heard this phrase. I'm certain it was not of my own making, but it captures the core of the work to which I believe we are called. Sometimes the barriers that exist between us aren't really about us—they are about the ghosts of past relationships with individuals or culture at large that get in the way.

As a chaplain, I find many persons want nothing to do with me. Actually, it's not me, although I know I can certainly rub my fair share of people the wrong way, but it's the title and what they think it means that they often avoid.

They expect judgment. They fear I'm coming to try to convert them or preach at them. They dread having the Bible "crammed down" their throats.

Certainly, some persons of faith have such zeal for what they believe to be the truth that they feel it is imperative to share that truth with others by whatever means necessary. I was raised in such a tradition and know it well. I understand the well-meaning intentions. I have seen the deep hearts filled with love that desperately want others to experience what they have found that means so much for them. I know, for me, however, that when I come from a place of desperation, there's little room for G-d to work, and I muck things up considerably!

As much as I understand where many are coming from in their quest to "share" their faith with others, I've also seen the tremendous damage that can be done when we presume to know what another's path should be and how they should get there. Especially when that sharing is not welcome, and is imposed in response to an invitation into someone's life and home to provide care.

As a hospice chaplain, I often hear the stories of many who have collected so much religious baggage that they avoid things of spirit altogether—the damage is profound. Sharing what works for oneself can be about connecting with another. Presuming that we know what they need is hubris. Judging them if they do not accept our version of truth is, I believe, plain and simple religious abuse. Breeching the ethical guidelines of the chaplaincy, which prohibits imposing one's religion on those in our care, is the ultimate damage of trust.

If a person's actual beliefs lead them to a place of atheism, agnosticism, humanism, etc. I have no need to convince them otherwise and I do not think of them as "less than" in any way. What I deeply regret and find exceedingly frustrating are those who do believe in a deity and want a connection but fear it because of the way they've been treated or disillusioned. Unfortunately, religion is sometimes used to divide us rather than draw us closer together in peace and love and understanding. My role is to seek ways to reassure and connect.

My introduction to "Mr. P" demonstrated that the divide was complicated by several factors.

He was a highly respected businessman who had done great things in this country, and his own homeland. I was asked to meet with the family, because they were facing an ethical challenge. The IV hydration this beloved patriarch was receiving was overloading his body, which could not process it any longer. With no way to make its way through his system, all the fluid was backing up around his heart and lungs, essentially drowning him.

He was unresponsive and could no longer make his own decisions, so the family was left to do so. He had just come into hospice services, so we were all trying to learn his and his family's needs. However, the doctor who had been following his case was clear that medically it would be irresponsible for him to continue administering fluids. He wanted to remove them immediately.

My hospice agency was a bit caught in the middle, left to deliver this news to a family whom we had just met. We advocated on behalf of the family, noting that they would need time to process this information or else it could turn into a disastrous situation. The doctor consented to give us the day.

When medical wisdom says that artificial feeding and hydration are no longer beneficial and are, in fact, harming the patient, the cognitive dissonance is often too great for loved ones in the face of grief. I'm from the South and in my hometown Chicken Spaghetti and other casseroles over-flowed a family's fridge during times of crisis. Feeding people equals love in most cultures. So to try to explain to the family it's time to stop doing so, that information just doesn't compute.

When there is a cultural or religious difference between the health-care staff and the family (in this case we had both), the distrust can simply be heightened. The daughter already was not happy I was there. Although I could not understand her words when she walked up and saw me speaking with her brother outside their father's room, I got the gist from her tone and expression, "What's the Christian doing here?"

I generally don't identify my belief system with patients and families. As a chaplain, my faith is to be in the background, keeping me grounded but not working its way into my conversation with those for whom I care. This is about them, not me.

But the term "chaplain" is assumed by most to mean "Christian" and they also think it means the same thing as "pastor," although neither are ex-clusively the case. Chaplains may be from any of the world's faith traditions and belief systems. Many have never lead a faith community or delivered a message in front of one. Most are educated and trained specifically to work with persons of all beliefs.

I do not wear jewelry that indicates my religion, as I do not want it to be an instant barrier. I wear, instead, a necklace. It is the very image used to develop the cover of this book, which many take to be a tree of life. For me, it's spiritual, but not religious, which I prefer for the sake of the work that I do.

But my badge says "Rev.," which is a pretty big give-away since that's used most often by Christians as the term for a faith leader. Whether she knew that, or made assumptions, I do not know, but the point is moot. She correctly assumed I was not Muslim and appeared to distrust my presence.

Having spent some time with me, the son knew that I knew their Imam from my involvement in the Interfaith Network in town. He had spoken with me long enough to know that I seek to train other chaplains on how to better understand all religions and be with persons of faiths other than their own in a respectful and helpful way.

He appeared pleasantly surprised when I asked if there was some way that I, as a non-Muslim and a female, could bring the Holy Recitations to his father. He smiled, and informed me of an application that would do that for me from my phone, with an imam reciting the Qur'an in Arabic. He even helped me bookmark the most important sura, or chapters, in the Qur'an for the end of life so I could simply play them on my phone for his father when I visited!

All the daughter knew was that she had been called to come to the facility because the doctor wanted to stop giving fluids to her dad, and when she walked up, a stranger who represents a different religion, a different culture, and who knows what all else, was part of the establishment discussing something that, in her mind, would hasten her father's death.

The brother appeared to speak in my defense, reassuring her my intentions were pure. The nurse was trying to explain the medical concerns to the family as they huddled outside their husband and father's door, but it was just all too much. The daughter would hear none of it.

Most of us can't absorb information like this quickly, and grief often comes out as conflict and resistance and anger. I don't blame people for this, I've done it, myself, and will likely do it, again. My job is to remember that and to try to understand the dynamics at hand rather than pathologizing their grief as anything other than just that—plain and simple human grief.

Realizing that this was not the time to try to build her trust in me, it seemed the best thing I could do was step back. Bad news from anyone is hard. Bad news from someone who seemingly represents what you already distrust—there's just no way for that to go well.

As the nurse who was the case manager for our hospice team tried to gently but clearly explain that the excess fluid was hurting their dad and husband, the energy was very tense. People were coming and going through the hall and Martha, our certified nurse aid, came by and waved as she went into the room to help clean the patient and change his linens.

The family insisted on standing by the door to his room, rather than a conference room, because they wanted to be close to him. Conversation was happening in three languages—the nurse speaking English to the family, the kids translating in fluid rhythms for their mother who did not speak English, and the nurse also trying to translate medical-jargon into plain English. Into the fray, came a small and sweet voice, "Excuse me?"

Martha had stepped back out of the patient's room and was addressing the family, "I'm sorry, but I'm wondering, is it permissible for me to trim your father's beard?"

The conversation in front of me came to a complete stop. After a long pause, the son answered quietly, "Yes, it is. My father is devout in his faith, but also takes great pride in his appearance, and preferred to keep his beard well-groomed. Thank you."

As Martha moved to walk back into the room, the daughter stopped her with a hand on her arm. Martha's hand was already on the door handle, "Wait," the daughter said. Martha turned back to the daughter and waited politely.

Looking at her brother, then mother, then to the nurse and to me, she finally looked back to Martha and said, "I have to know, how did you know to ask whether it was permissible?"

Martha's shoulders slumped slightly for a moment and her gaze cast down to the floor, before coming back to meet the daughter's own. Both women's eyes were now misting. Speaking with deep and sincere regret, Martha answered, "Because there was a time when I did not know to ask, and I trimmed the beard of a Muslim man for whom it was not permissible." She swallowed hard, "I felt awful, and I pray I never make that mistake, again."

In silence, Martha smiled kindly at the family, and went in to complete her duties. A long moment passed before the daughter took a deep breath, squared her shoulders to face both the nurse and me, and said, "Please tell me, again, what does your doctor wish to do?"

The entire conversation changed. All our best intentions and admittedly seasoned skills in working with persons from all faiths and cultures had done nothing to help gain this family's trust. But our co-worker's seemingly simple yet deeply profound gesture of respect and honor for the family's faith and culture did in seconds what all our best verbal knowledge had not been able to do in over an hour.

The bridge of trust was securely fastened, and we could all now meet in the middle of it to reason together what was most caring for their dad.

When others know that we are willing to sit with them as they are, then we earn the trust that allows us to walk beside them, and even serve as a bit of a guide in uncharted territory. But first, we must sit. I'm grateful that Martha could do just that.

I'm Trying to Die Here

In any stressful field, "gallows" humor—grim and ironic in the face of challenging circumstances—is a way of coping. I was horrified when I first learned of it. In one of my first jobs, I was working with seasoned and highly skilled social workers, psychologists, and counselors whom I saw as the epitome of professionalism and compassion. And then I attended my first "staffing" meeting.

Every other week, we met to discuss challenging cases, go over treatment plans with our supervisors, and seek support from our colleagues. I was absolutely horrified by some of the jokes they cracked during this meeting, and in my immature self-righteousness, I became quite indignant.

A woman I greatly respected pulled me aside and said, "Look, kid, if you want to make it in this field, hearing and seeing some of the worst challenges that kids should never have to face, you've got to find some way to offload the horror or it will eat you alive. We have the utmost respect for the patients, but if you can't laugh at circumstances from time to time, you'll burn out within a year."

She was right.

I learned there is a difference between respecting the pain and process of patients, (who are real people), and laughing behind closed doors in the face of trauma. There is a tenuous balance between being human and being professional. Both are allowed and both must be curtailed to some degree. In that middle ground we find the place where we can survive tough times without becoming hardened, bitter, and uncaring.

I even came across an article in a nursing journal in the early 1990s that researched the nurses who found ways to use humor to cope verses those who did not. Burnout rates and depression were much higher for those who could not make room in their professional demeanors to find space to laugh. I'm still learning the balance of irreverence and honor—twenty years later.

Most people expect explanations, reassurances of "G-d's will," and the like when the chaplain arrives. Therefore, they are often taken aback when, instead of platitudes, I walk in and say, "Wow…this sucks!" Thankfully, it comes out as compassionate rather than flippant, because I think they can truly hear the care and regret in my voice.

After a confused double-take at my name badge, "Yep, it says 'Rev. Dr.'", they laugh and confess, "Well yeah, it does!" And then they relax and drop the "Sunday School" language and tell me what's really going on in their hearts and minds. From that genuine place, we can talk about their fears, their worries, and do a crash course in "Hospice 101." I help them understand what to expect from hospice and the disease process in the weeks and months ahead.

They ask questions again and again, and we patiently answer them over and over, because we know that when persons are under extreme stress, the brain can only absorb so much information at once, and it often takes hearing things a dozen times for the concepts to sink in for the entire family. As we pull the fear gremlins out from under the table, where they're gnawing on our ankles, and lay them out in the open to talk about them, it's amazing how much smaller they seem.

Besides, we can do something with the gremlins we can see. It's the ones we hear snickering around the corner out of sight that can wreck havoc on our imaginations and haunt our waking moments. We want everyone to have a better idea of what to expect. We are there to take over the "heavy lifting" medically, so they can relax and settle into a new "normal." Once they realize that hospice staff is there to respect their home, wishes, beliefs, and dignity—they can see that we are able to help life return to some sense of normalcy for them.

Our goal is to maximize quality of life for whatever quantity naturally remains for everyone involved. Knowing that we are the interlopers, we strive to adapt to the personality and culture of the person receiving hospice as well as that of their entire family. We pay attention. We listen to stories. We pick up cues and share them with our team members so we can all work to provide as little intrusion as possible as guests in the home (whether "home" is one's own or a room in a facility).

Sometimes, people surprise us and make it incredibly clear exactly how they want their process to go, so there's absolutely no need to guess on our part!

A woman named "Carol" came onto our hospice service. I was told her daughter, "Wendy," was at the skilled nursing facility at her mom's bedside. As I walked into the darkened room, Wendy made a "hushing" motion with her finger to her lips then waved for me to come on in.

We tiptoed to a corner of the room and talked in hushed tones, feeling our voices were masked by the box fan blowing directly onto Carol's bed. I could see her slight but tall frame under the covers, the lavender flowers on her white cotton nightgown, and the rapid rise and fall of the short and shallow breaths, indicating she was perhaps within hours to days of death.

Every person's body and illness are unique, so there is no crystal ball to determine exactly when "it" will happen. Families often want to know, which is understandable. I tell them that our nurses will update them as they see changes in their loved one, but that we hesitate to give specific time frames. I assure them, "If we tell you it will be two minutes and it winds up being two years, you'll be upset with us for leaving you waiting for so long. If we say two years and death comes in two minutes, you'll be upset with us because you weren't prepared."

But there are fairly typical stages that can be seen over the course of months, weeks, days, hours, and minutes. Many resources are available online and in print that are incredibly helpful in preparing persons for what to expect. Barbara Karnes has written one booklet that is particularly helpful called *Gone From My Sight: The Dying Experience*. Some know it as, "That blue hospice book," because it is such an industry standard. To date, it is one of the clearest and best resources I know of to help persons understand what to expect during the dying process in clear and gentle terms.

According to the nurse case manager overseeing our hospice team for Carol's case, she was showing signs of being "actively dying," which indicates death may occur within a few hours to two or three days. As we stood huddled quietly in the corner, Wendy told me of her mother's very rapid disease progression after the time of diagnosis. She said her mother was always a very practical, "cut and dried" kind of woman. She was a real character, to hear her daughter tell it, and had declared after leaving the doctor's office the last time that she had decided to "get this whole thing over with."

I was mid-sentence questioning Wendy about what exactly Carol had meant by this, when Carol raised up her head and interrupted us in a clear, loud, and obviously irritated voice, "Do you mind? I'm trying to DIE here!"

If I had been mid-drink, the liquid would have immediately found its way out of my nose and halfway across the room! Carol answered the question I hadn't finished getting out of my mouth. She had decided to, "Get this whole thing over with" and make fast work of dying.

"Sorry, Mother," the daughter squeaked out, while we held our breath like two scolded kids. We barely made it out to the hall and closed the heavy wooden door before we both lost it, howling in laughter.

We wound up on the hall floor, leaning against the wall, wiping tears from our eyes. When our giggles finally subsided, the daughter heaved that final sigh that comes after a long release of laughter, turned to me, straightened up in a cordial manner and said, "Yes, chaplain, you were asking…?"

Fresh peals of laughter rang off the walls. The daughter's tears slowly came to be released as soft sobs. She leaned her head on my shoulder as I put an arm around her and we just sat there as she released even more emotion. Carol was ready to be done. Wendy wasn't quite there, yet, but wanted to honor her mom's wishes. Patients live with illness 24/7 with no escape, so often they are ready to die far before the rest of us are ready to let go.

Finally, when it seemed as if she had found a resting place, I said, "So, around this time, I'm usually asking folks to tell me about their mother, but I think that was just answered quite nicely!" We giggled, again. "So tell me about you…" I continued, "…how are you?"

She sat up, finding a spare corner on her crumpled tissue to wipe her nose, and started telling me stories. We laughed some more. She cried some more. She shared her feelings and beliefs and fears and struggles. As Wendy talked, she came to terms more and more with what had happened so quickly that her emotions had not yet had time to catch up. Carol had her process. Wendy needed to have hers.

In the face of the gallows, life was still happening. Her mother was exactly as she always had been, for better or worse. Carol was no saint, as none of us are. She was beautifully imperfect, impetuous, and petulant, feisty and funny, witty and impatient, determined and tenacious. Wendy was able to share all of it in a way that worked for her, and we made sure to do so without interrupting her mother's determined work to, "Get this thing over and done with!"

The saintly, somber, prescribed process that many believe death "should" look like wouldn't have worked for Carol. After decades with her mother's personality, anything different might have been too much for Wendy to handle, I don't know. But what I do know is that Carol was getting to die on her own terms in her own way.

Thankfully, we could all let it be the process she needed and find humor in it all, as well as space for grief for Wendy in the midst of the whole messy, imperfect, all too real experience, which is exactly as it should be.

Anarchy

The admissions nurse asked me to join her at the family's home in a small, rural town. I was told she was Catholic and wanted a priest, but the priest wasn't available and the nurse thought that talking with the chaplain sooner rather than later would be helpful. The patient agreed.

When I arrived, this relatively young woman, especially by hospice standards at 67, appeared tired and quite anxious as she lay on the couch in the middle of the living room. I got to know the family a bit, as her adult children were present. They were all staying at the home with her and their father, almost around the clock, leaving only to work as much as they had to and pick up kids from school.

Her children were very sweet with her. There were obviously some unspoken issues floating around, but poking and digging for those isn't our job. We simply provide space and offer invitations for patients and families to tell us whatever they are comfortable sharing whenever they are ready to share it. They decide whether and when to trust us to receive it. We must follow their lead and respect their process and timing.

As her adult children wandered off to care for the grandbabies and leave for work, the everyday bustle of activity had an easy feel to it. They were certainly all sad. They didn't want to accept what the doctor finally got around to telling them after months of hemming and hawing: the cancer wasn't going away, and had even spread.

Her husband didn't want to hear it. He couldn't go there, yet. He needed more time to bring up other ways of coping so he could let go of the one protecting him now—denial. Like many medical personnel, the doctor couldn't bring himself to say the words he knew they definitely didn't want to hear (we're working to change that dynamic!).

So for months they drove 120 miles round trip every other week in the family's old station wagon to be told nothing, in so many words, and propped up to pretend another couple of weeks. Perhaps the physician meant it as emotional palliation, keeping them comfortable by avoiding the honest conversation as long as possible, until the patient finally was the one who had the courage to confront the doctor with the truth he couldn't say, "I'm dying, aren't I?"

When he couldn't answer, but only looked down at his shoes, and then handed them a referral to hospice, the patient thanked him graciously and made the drive home, knowing she wouldn't leave it, at least not alive, again. We came in a couple of days later.

Not having time to prepare themselves for the inevitable or to receive all the support they needed and deserved from hospice, the family was reeling and angry with the doctor, with life, and with G_d. They were trying hard to find their way past it so as to not rob their mother of peace in what were clearly becoming her final days. The sudden screeching of emotional brakes as they shifted abruptly from aggressively treating cancer to aggressively treating the symptoms of cancer through hospice care was simply too much to take in so quickly.

As the house settled from the after-school activity and then the dinner hour, the nurse spoke quietly on the phone from a chair on the front porch to avoid making more "clinical" noise in their home. She called the pharmacy and medical equipment company to get everything the patient and family needed for the patient to stay there comfortably. We would stay as long as was needed to get them settled and comfortable before we left. As the nurse made her calls, the patient's spouse dozed off in his recliner. COPS was on the television in the background with the sound lowered. The patient and I talked quietly, finally in private.

She spoke of her faith journey from childhood to present day. Her story was fairly typical, especially once the cancer intruded on their household schedule and their emotional and physical energy.

The priest they knew left to go to another parish.

They did not know the new priest, and no one had thought to send him out to see her as the illness kept them away from weekly services. The family felt hurt by their faith family allowing them to fall through the cracks like that, "But honestly, Chaplain, I understand things happen and really, I don't have time to be holding grudges," she admitted. I agreed to call the priest and ask him to come later in the week, at her request.

For now, she spoke of not sleeping. Those of us on the team who are not nurses or doctors do not tread into their territory, but as a cohesive team we do ask questions so we can pass along helpful information to our medical colleagues. I asked if there were some symptoms causing her sleeplessness. There were none.

So I asked how she felt about the dark. She said she was never afraid of the dark, even as a child, but now…. She couldn't explain it, but she knew she didn't like being asleep or alone at night.

I assured her this was common. "Activity and noise during the day speak to us of security and comfort with our loved ones around us. At night, when they're asleep, and we're alone, some people find that they worry death will come and take them when no one is watching, and the thought of going to sleep is overwhelmed by thoughts of not waking up."

She visibly relaxed as the words sank in, and she was reassured she was neither crazy nor alone. We talked about how she was coping with this, how her faith was helping her with her fears.

Then her youngest son walked in, kissed her cheek, and shook my hand hello before joining us on the other side of her on the couch with his arm around her shoulders. He worked the late shift, so he slept during the day, went to work, then came home when the others went to sleep and stayed up with her all night. He took off early this evening to come meet us, at her request.

I asked what they did during the night, and she seemed horrified when he told me they watched back-to-back episodes of "Sons of Anarchy," a mature-themed television drama series about a young father involved in a motorcycle gang. She blushed and glanced at me, then not-so-subtly reminded him I was the chaplain and elbowed him gently in the ribs.

When my response was, "Cool! I've heard about it but have never seen it. Catch me up, what is it about?

She heaved a huge sigh of relief. The non-religious son visibly relaxed with me, and suddenly became animated as he described characters and plotlines and episodes. He had been polite, but only now warmed up to our conversation. She beamed as she watched him talk. He could have been reciting pizza crust recipes and she would have looked at him with just the same sense of adoration and sweet pride.

As I asked questions about which characters they liked most and least, what they loved about the show, etc., he talked up a storm. He loved the show. She loved him. It became clear that he identified with the main character who is faced ethical dilemmas as he tries to balance his responsibilities to his two worlds. He wanted to do the right thing, but wasn't always so sure what exactly that was.

It also became clear that she cared nothing about the show. She cared about sharing something with him. This was her way of connecting with her hard to reach, quiet son just as she had when he was a child and teen.

She said she knew he was tired and had changed his schedule to accommodate her fears, and how much she appreciated it. She spoke of her worries about him, the designated black sheep of the family who did not get along well with his father, and sometimes his siblings, and what was going to happen to him when she was gone.

It gave us room to explore that relationship and her worries and fears for him, as well as her pride in him. Between retellings of episodes, the stories and love and concern for him slowly flowed out.

They cried. They hugged. They whispered their love quietly to one another and made promises—he to "get right" and "straighten up", and she to always love and watch over him. It appeared to be healing for them both, and was one of those precious intimate moments we are privileged to witness as we help hold safe space to encourage such conversations to happen if that's where they want to go. We prayed for peace and guidance, comfort and wisdom for the entire family before I left for the evening.

When I saw them again two days later to check in, they told me they both fell asleep that night only halfway through the first episode, sitting up on the couch, she with her head on his shoulder and he with his head resting gently on hers.

Despite the crick in their necks the next morning, they said it was the best night's sleep they had had in months. Both of their fears and worries had been shared with each other and released, and the patient said she finally felt at peace.

She died the next day.

I participate in several on-line professional forums designed for sharing information and ideas that allow us to grapple with challenging scenarios together. A participant from one particular group comprised of professional and "lay" chaplains who work in ministry questioned whether the rest of us had "a problem" with the violent and/or sexual shows some families choose to watch on television while a patient is dying.

I thought of and shared the above story and the lessons I learned and was reminded of from this mother and son.

First, I have to check my assumptions and judgments at the door. As soon as I believe I know what their experience should look like, I've set myself up as the expert on their life. That is disrespectful to the ethic of autonomy and dignity we in clinical professions are called to honor.

This may be exactly what the patient is accustomed to hearing in the background so, as a familiar sound, it may be comforting to him or her and speak of "home" and a normal routine. Interfering with that is none of my business. Who am I to decide that I know more than do they what they need?

If the family is using the television as a buffer from reality, or to stay in denial, I must not deem that a pathology. Defenses and stages of processing are there for a reason, and folks often move through them naturally when they are ready, with little to no intervention. For me to assume that I know when they are or "should be" ready to let go of a distraction would be hubris on my part.

If the volume is loud and distracting to me in my visit, I may respectfully ask permission for it to be lowered so that I can truly hear them.

If the patient appears agitated by the noise or content, then that's a whole other issue, as we are called to advocate for patients needs and rights. But if I have a "problem" with their choices, then I am the one who has a problem.

In those times, I get to check in to see what is getting stirred up inside of me and why. Am I casting judgment? If so, why? Whatever I find that is going on inside of me, I get to deal with that so I can be with them, aware of my own stuff, and watch for how it is getting in the way of their process.

If it is the case that an aide, for example, has turned the channel in a patient's room to what he or she wants to hear rather than something the patient would normally choose, we can advocate for the patient, find out what shows he or she likes, and request those shows be chosen when the television is on.

But what I learned that day as I listened about Sons of Anarchy while COPS was on in the background was that such moments can also become an opening. I walked away changed as a result of that experience.

If I had missed that chance to see and hear her and her family, I would have failed at my job that day. Thankfully, I was in a good place to have words that opened hearts and minds and conversation; that built a bridge rather than a barrier.

Whether someone needs silence or the sound of Sons of Anarchy in their ears as they live until their end of life, who am I to do anything but express acceptance and even curiosity? A conversation about a television show proved to be a surrogate conversation they hadn't been able to have directly. I hope I never judge another's process, and in so doing totally miss what they need to say.

Popcorn and Dominoes

We really don't know how to do this "death" thing much anymore. More accurately, we don't think we know how to do it because we've forgotten that this is simply a part of life and we really can't "do it wrong." We've forgotten that we know how to do this.

As I said at the beginning of this book, fortunately, we are coming back to ourselves, and hospice is helping to make that happen. As much as anything, we hospice staff help people remember what they already know and help them trust and follow their gut about how to be and what to do. All that is really needed is to show up. Period.

We frequently walk in and find families more than a bit stunned or overwhelmed and in shock. This whole experience is new to them and they don't have a clear road map. So the scene I see when I walk in and a patient is in the stage of actively dying often looks like this: Family and friends standing or sitting around the bedside motionless, saying nothing, and staring at their loved one. They appear lost. And I get it.

Sometimes, we need the silence and stillness as the shock wears off and we grapple to wrap our heads and hearts around what is happening. Someone can be sick and in and out of the hospital for months or years and when the time finally comes, no matter how well prepared we think we are, death still tends to catch us off guard to some extent. We need time to let our psyches "catch up" to reality.

Other times, the silence and stillness is less about this, and more about feeling way out of our element and not wanting to, "get it wrong." So we sit. We stare. We wait. If this way of waiting suits the needs of the patient and family, I'm fine with that. I've no judgments about it.

But if it's more about being frozen by a lack of knowing what to do, I believe it robs us of some rich moments of being with the person who is still living, even as they lay dying. These are moments that we do not want to miss.

That is why we encourage loved ones to say and do everything they need to say and do while they can, even seconds before death, or in the hours following, so they will be less likely to regret not having one last hug or one more, "I love you." Many patients wind up in hospital beds, even in their own home, for comfort and ease of care since the beds move heads and feet and bodies up and down as needed. Showing families how to operate the controls and rails so they can get closer to their loved one may be, single handedly, one of the greatest spiritual interventions I do!

I want irrational and unintentional barriers cleared away to make room for whatever needs to happen. I've seen grown men and women snuggle up to their momma or daddy or spouse or sibling or friend or child in the last hours—one more time for kisses and hugs as they try to memorize their touch and scent and the connection that gives them comfort.

We try to "read" the situation. We offer education about what to expect and we model and teach how to be with someone when, for instance, feeding pudding or pushing sips of water becomes unsafe, or unwelcomed by the patient.

That is when we show them mouth swabs that patients may suck on to get a taste of that Dr. Pepper, which gives them pleasure, in a way their bodies can handle. We pull out lotion and discuss where and how it might feel best for it to be applied. We soak washcloths in cool water and caress cheeks, necks, and brows with it as the body loses its ability to control its internal thermostat.

But we must remain cognizant that such hands-on interactions could be strange and unnatural for some families and even patients! We must be sensitive to this dynamic, and honor it, as well.

I was called to a home in an historic part of town on a Sunday afternoon. I walked in and found the kids and grandkids of the family matriarch, who was in her early nineties, standing in her bedroom in their childhood home where she had lived for over 60 years (independently until two weeks before).

The hardwood floors creaked as I walked across them to join the admissions nurse, (who was there to bring the patient onto hospice services), and the family at the bedside. Mine were the only feet making any noise in the house, other than the sound of her gentle but rapid breathing. The family was so still, it seemed they, too were barely breathing.

They nodded quiet hellos and then resumed their posts, surrounding her bed and staring at this tiny but seemingly powerful woman who could not seem to die. All signs indicated her body was ready, but she couldn't seem to "settle," is the best way I know to describe it. She did not seem anxious or agitated, but she didn't seem relaxed, either. Something was up, but I wasn't quite sure what it was.

I asked a few questions to do a quickie assessment, gathering as much information as I could to let me know how to best help them, without intruding too much at this delicate time. They answered politely and openly, in hushed voices, apparently not wanting to disturb the beloved queen of that castle, and family.

They were grateful for her, spoke fondly of her and her life, admired her strength and quiet love and determination to care well for them all. They recounted how she easily accepted her sudden diagnosis and rapid decline in that simple down-to-earth way that takes life on life's terms without complaint or fuss.

She was simply grateful, as were they, that she had over 90 years with exceptional health up until the previous two weeks. So they were confused about why she was lingering after having a consistent and rapid decline the previous 24 hours.

Nothing seemed undone or unresolved, but there was an uneasiness present that was palpable, although unclear. As they described this proud, independent, determined, spit-fire of a 5'2" woman, it finally came to me: "So, you say she has always been proud and independent. Would you say she was also a pretty private person?"

"Very!" said various family members, almost in stereo.

I considered this. "I'm guessing, then, that she doesn't normally sleep or relax with a room full of people standing over her and watching her, right?"

They grinned sheepishly and shrugged that they guessed not.

"I don't mean to say anything negative at all about what you're doing. You can stay right here, absolutely as long as you need to do so. But when you're ready, it might help her relax into death to be given that space she's normally accustomed to having, alone in her home."

The family turned back to their mother and, grandmother, and their concentration frowns indicated they were considering this. It seemed to ring true for them that this might very well be the issue.

After giving them several moments for this to sink in, I went on, "Brain scans indicate our senses of smell and hearing are the last to leave us when we die. I'm curious, then, about what smells and sounds would normally be in this house when the whole family is together like this, which might feel more natural and relaxing to her?"

Without missing a beat, the eldest grandson laughed and said, "Popcorn and dominoes!"

"Forty-two?" I asked.

They all nodded and murmured, "Yes!"

"Well gimme that 6-4!" I exclaimed.

They all laughed at the familiar trash-talking line used by those who play that competitive dominoes game.

"In all seriousness, please stay just like this as long as you need. When you're ready, the nurse will stay right here to make sure she's comfortable, and you can give her what's familiar and may just help her let go."

The nurse and I stepped out of the room to give them privacy. Slowly, over the next five minutes, they each wandered into the kitchen, where I joined them, as the nurse sat quietly in a darkened corner of the patient's bedroom.

In another five minutes, they had relaxed the party into full swing. The second bag of thankfully not burnt popcorn was dinging and steaming its way enticingly out of the microwave and into large plastic bowls, wafting all over the house.

The "thwack" and "crack" of dominoes slapping the table and clattering together staccatoed between laughter and good-natured banter and teasing over players' bids and hands around the dining room table, echoing off the walls. I swear, the voices of other generations of this family who had gathered here just like this joined them in that moment.

Kids were running around snagging handfuls of popcorn before running off to chase after their older cousins in the house. Twilight had fallen outside the huge plate glass windows, overlooking her six-decades old rose bushes and the street view that they all knew so very well.

Eleven minutes after the last family member kissed her cheek goodnight and resumed life as had always been normal for them around her kitchen, she died peacefully.

The nurse came to the doorway of the kitchen, smiled softly, and nodded the news. The adults and teenagers grew quiet for a few moments, then one daughter raised her glass and the others joined her with both chardonnay and red solo cups of grape Kool-Aid to toast the woman who brought them all to that table, and taught them how to live around it.

Now, she taught them again, about how to let death come just as easily and naturally as their laughter.

There was one more round of tears and kisses, and then the game and play resumed as we awaited the funeral home. They were ready. She was ready. It was okay. They just didn't want to be disrespectful at what television shows and movies tell us is this somber, quiet, sacred time. And it is.

But it's also about continuing to live the life we've always known, always wanted, and that's always carried us through, by allowing the familiar to walk us right up to the doorway, which otherwise can seem so scary because it is unknown. When we remove the taboos of what we think should be and pay attention to that which life calls us to, we find our way. Trust your instincts. They rarely lead us astray.

Unexpected Gifts

Our hearts break when children face challenges. Pediatric hospice and palliative care can bring us to our collective knees, but not simply from sadness, as many believe. Children bring a powerful sense of resilience and matter-of-fact simplicity to the natural rhythms of life. When that life is ending far too soon, and those rhythms seem excruciatingly unnatural, the voices of the children are often the ones comforting and reassuring us grown-ups with their sense of acceptance and peace and reassurance.

We train persons to never say things such as, "God needed another angel," or any other such cliché or platitude to try to explain away any tragedy—especially when it involves a child. If a grieving person finds comfort in such statements, let them be the ones to speak them. But if we try to put a spin on their pain, we may do enormous damage to a grieving heart. It is natural for us to have difficulty facing such sadness. However, let us be mindful that if we fear the pain, or try too hard to push it away, we may miss the gifts of being with what is—with those who are experiencing it—even when it hurts like hell.

While we struggle to come to terms with the inexplicable and unimaginable—with the death of a child—their hands are often the very ones leading us through to a deeper and more openhearted space, even as our hearts break.

And when our own hearts are breaking, we can rely on others from our hospice community for guidance. Some of the most memorable moments of my career have been spent with the phenomenal group of professionals who formed the Chaplain Development Committee I co-founded through the Texas New Mexico Hospice Organization. They have become some of my closest friends and most respected colleagues. This work is a joy—and I won't deny that it does have its challenges. Having a "tribe" with whom to commiserate, share challenges and triumphs; by whom we can run ideas and questions, and who we trust always love us and has our backs, regardless of our mistakes and flaws, is something I wish every person could experience.

I first heard Rev. Dr. Rodney Bolejack share this story when we were the co-leaders of an all-day training in Grand Junction, Colorado several years ago, just as my training and consulting business was getting started. I can see Rodney, the tender and delightfully playful and boyish grandfather that he is, sitting in the dirt or scrambling on his knees to meet this young girl exactly as she needed. My heart swells when I hear Rodney describe the knowing hands of the nurse doing a careful examination in a most unorthodox way, again because that is what was needed. Her story is a testament to the wisdom of children.

Bradie

I first met Bradie on a pile of dirt clods. She was four. She was a hospice patient. She had a cancer that first appeared in the bone at her knee. At age two, her leg was amputated at the knee. Her prosthesis was helpful, but often more of a nuisance to her. I would soon learn that she was indeed independent, opinionated, and quite a fireball.

She was also quite weary of doctors and people who wore scrubs. Her reputation and her fighting spirit were known across the often-visited halls of the local hospital. Once, while waiting to see her doctor, Bradie played in the children's toy area of the waiting room. A pediatrician, some-one who had not treated her, but like so many had heard of her, saw Bradie, confirmed who she was with the receptionist, and came out to meet her.

He approached her, kneeled beside her and extended his hand for a handshake. "Hello, Bradie. My name is Dr. Gray. I have heard so much about you and I want to meet you."

Without missing a beat, Bradie responded, "I'm sorry doctor, but you don't have an appointment. Please get one and come back later."

That was classic Bradie. And the entire 400-bed hospital had heard of this encounter within the hour.

I wore shorts and a polo shirt to meet Bradie. I hoped to not appear too "official" and to make at least a friendly connection with Bradie. On the days our nurse visited her, she wore a bathing suit under her scrubs. Together, they would play in the water and have swim lessons. All the while, the nurse was doing a physical exam. And more—they were forming a bond. Soon, so would I.

After meeting Bradie's mom, she took me to the back door and pointed to Bradie, playing on a pile of dirt clods left from the excavation for the above ground pool. She called to Bradie to introduce me. Bradie didn't look up but continued placing clods in an unpredictable pattern. I sat beside her on top of the sunbaked clods. "Hey, Bradie. Whatcha doing?"

"I'm finding dinosaur bones!" she said, emphatically.

"Cool!" And as she picked up a clod I asked, "What's that one?"

She held it up, then placed it down with purpose as she said, "That's part of his neck."

"Ohhhh, I see."

She picked up another and again I inquired of this four-year-old paleontologist, "And what's that one?"

She identified it quickly and with a bit of a tone in her voice that suggested I must be quite ignorant to not know what I was looking at. "It's part of his back."

"Of course. I see that now. Hey, can I help?"

"Sure."

I picked up a dirt clod and examined with a few thoughtful "Hmmmmm's." Then I handed it to Bradie and said proudly, "Look at this. I found part of his leg."

"No silly! That's part of his tail!" Of course, she was right. She was Bradie!

Over the next months I visited Bradie, I became acquainted with her wonderful mom and dad, grandparents, and some of the extended family. Bradie's family was amazing. They were filled will so much love, so much pain, so much faith, and an awareness of the inevitable and approaching death of their Bradie.

I visited Bradie often. We had a developing friendship. Most of the time it was casual small talk. I spent time with her mom and dad and visiting relatives, offering support and spiritual reflection. There was always a story to tell about Bradie.

On one particular day that I called to offer a visit, Bradie was staying across town at her grandmother's home. I was invited over to spend time with Bradie and visit with her grandmother. It was a warm Texas day so I put on shorts, a casual shirt, and my tennis shoes and made the trek to see her. When I arrived, Bradie invited me to watch a, "princess movie," with her in her grandmother's bedroom.

I hesitated to intrude on such a private place, but Grandmother's head nod reassured me, and off we went. Grandmother soon followed and served us Dr. Peppers to enjoy during the movie. Bradie giggled and pointed out key moments of the movie to me.

When it was over, I asked what she wanted to do next. She shrugged and then her eyes lit up and she said, "Let's race." There was a straight path from a bathroom doorway on one side of the room to a doorway opening into a living room on the other side. The thresholds made perfect finish lines.

Bradie declined to put on her prosthesis for this sprint. She would run on her knee and her stump. I would be on my knees. I teased that she had better be speedy because I was fast on my knees. She grinned and took a ready position.

"On your mark...set...GO!" Bradie really was fast! I trailed just far enough behind to be able to reach out and tag her so she'd know I was closing in. She squealed and kept going!

"I'm gonna beat you, Bradie!" And she squealed again. Of course, she beat me.

She celebrated her victory by saying, "Let's race again!" So across the room we ran, knees and stump thumping the floor, tagging and squealing and laughing!

"Again!" she celebrated and she took off before I could say, "Get set..."

I was really close this time and she squealed and laughed all the louder. This time, when we got to the threshold she did not stop but continued into the living room. And, I followed. She ran past a coffee table to a sofa that she climbed to the top of in one swift motion. I recall thinking that her grandmother might disapprove of my climbing onto the back of the sofa, so I scooted between it and the coffee table.

When Bradie reached the end of the sofa she turned abruptly, looked down on me from her lofty position, and said, "Did you know that I am dying?"

I was caught off guard. This is what I had been waiting for. This is why I had worn shorts and tennis shoes and played with dinosaur bones and watched movies and engaged in small talk. Even so, it surprised me.

"Yes, Bradie, that's what I have heard. What do you think it will be like?"

She pondered the question a moment and then said, "Oh.... like Ariel."

Fortunately, I had a young girl who watched Disney movies at our house. I was familiar with Ariel from *The Little Mermaid*. And, I was struck that Bradie could relate to Ariel who sang a song about her dreams. She wanted to go, "...up to the street where the people have feet." Bradie was speaking of heaven where she believed her healing would come and her body would be whole again.

"What do you think God is like?" I inquired.

"Oh, like King Triton!"

He was a kind, caring, powerful father to Ariel and ruler of the oceans. "And what will you say to him, Bradie?"

"Not much. I'm just going to sit in his lap." She had captured, for her own understanding, an image of heaven and healing, of God, and of peace and comfort.

Months passed. Bradie grew weaker and then stayed in bed most of the time. She never mentioned Ariel to me again. I had received an unexpected gift in an unexpected moment. It is a gift I treasure even now. I was welcomed into the heart and soul of a child.

When Bradie died, it was a stormy, rainy night. We were all there in her home: parents, grandparents, nurse, social worker, chaplain, and her long time pediatric oncologist. We had each received our own gifts from Bradie. We shared stories and comforted each other. And when the thunder became loud, Bradie's mom announced, "That's Bradie! She has her leg back. She's climbing trees and when Jesus comes to get her down she jumps down, lands with a bang and runs to the next tree with Jesus still chasing her."

This was indeed a beautiful image! Bradie, in heaven, healed whole, and having a blast! And, she was being playfully chased by Jesus. Or, perhaps, it was King Triton.

Rodney shared this with me, and the workshop participants at our training, that he learned numerous lessons from Bradie and her family. He learned how important it is for us to listen for and learn to speak the language of those with whom we work. As we do, we call upon our patience and ability to simply be present in a way that helps patients develop a sense of trust in us, and our relationship with them.

From that place of understanding and presence, we can find ways to adapt to the needs and values and fears of the patient, and not be so hung up on thinking there is only one "right way" to be with them. We can let go of the "uniforms" that may make us feel more legitimate and respectable and wear shorts and tennis shoes and bathing suits to let this time be about the patient, because it is all about them!

As we do, we can expect unexpected gifts to find us, and hopefully the amazing human beings whom we seek to serve.

Thank you to Bradie, and to all our tiny and powerful teachers and their parents, for letting us have the life-changing honor of sitting at your feet.

Rev. Dr. Rodney Bolejack has served as a hospice spiritual care counselor since 1990. Rodney co-founded and serves as the previous chairperson for the Denton Area Partnership for End-of-Life Care. He is a volunteer chaplain for the Lake Cities Fire Department and frequently presents on healthcare topics for local, state, and national organizations. He is the recipient of the Chuck Meyer Award for Excellence in End-of-Life Care and amongst his greatest joys he lists spending time with his, "better-than-average grandchildren."

TNMHO is one of the many state organizations around the country that supports, educates, and connects hospices in order to promote ethical practices and excellence in care.

The Chaplain Development Committee formed in response to the need for more clinical training for spiritual care counselors and was approved and supported by the TNMHO Board of Directors. It met almost weekly for a year to conduct needs assessment surveys and develop a training curriculum for hospice chaplains. The training went viral and nurses, social workers, physicians, and the like, all began to attend. When other states, and even the National Hospice and Palliative Care Organization, began to call and request the training, the group graciously supported me in turning the curriculum into my own business (Carla Cheatham Consulting Group, LLC).

The Gifts We Cannot Refuse

She said she began teaching when she was five years old. She'd come home from school and teach the other smaller children what she had learned. I visited her in the room she had designed around her favorite bright colors when she and her husband built their house. It was intended to be a comfortable and cozy place to sit and be when the time came that she could do little else.

At that point, her son and daughter-in-law had moved in with her. She was able to greet visitors with gratitude and grace in that room. She refused to feel sorry for herself or be in a bad mood. Gratitude and love oozed out of her pores. She frequently said, "I'm happy to be who I am, as I am, where I am, and with whom I am," and she meant it.

I asked her how she came to be so positive. She told me that one day, when she was four years old, she was looking at family photos and saw one of herself at two years of age, sitting in a field in a small rocking chair in front of a row of sunflowers. As she looked at this picture of her younger self, she began to cry. When her mother, whom she described as, "a beautiful and phenomenal woman," asked her why, she pointed to the picture and said, "Because I'm in this big field all alone." Her mother replied, "Oh, darling, you are never alone. G-d is always with you."

At four years old, she said that truth sank into the core of her being, and, "G-d wrapped me up so tightly in that assurance, that from that moment on I never, ever, in my entire life, ever doubted it or felt alone or afraid."

She radiated that assurance of love onto everyone who entered her room. She gifted me by allowing me to sing to her when her voice could no longer form the notes, and pray for her when her mind developed difficulty finding words. As I pulled back from hugging her goodbye, her tear-filled smile said it all—adoration, joy, and the profound and deep gratitude she always spoke to me, when she could, before I left.

Knowing it might be our last moment, I placed my hand on her cheek and said sincerely, "Thank you for sharing your love with me." Then, when I thought my heart couldn't fill any more from our connection, she reached up with her soft, gnarled fingers, and found my cheek as well. She opened and closed her mouth a few times; breath escaped each time as she tried to find and press out words. Finally, I said, "It's ok. I know…," and just knelt there, as we explored one another's eyes and soaked in the experience of a truly intimate connection.

We try hard not to "take" from the patients and families with whom we work. It is a boundary to protect them from being taken advantage of, either intentionally or accidentally, by those who provide care. But quite often, there are gifts we receive that have nothing to do with money, possessions, or sexual indiscretion. It is about connection with another who teaches us, inspires us, simply loves us and shines such that we cannot help but be touched, even if we try.

Those are the moments that keep us coming back, and they are the very things that prompt most of us to smile and shake our heads in the negative when we are told how hard this work must be. Beautiful, poignant, sweet, tender, funny, inspiring…I don't mean to be cavalier or to minimize the challenges, the compassion fatigue (it used to be called burnout), the long hours—the sadness. But we look for ways to hold space for all of this without carrying it with us. If we can find that balance, then it is a joy.

When our compassion does tire out, because we are human and it does happen, then we can find ways to renew ourselves for the short term, or even the long term in a new or different field. But when I ask my colleagues, "hard" isn't usually how they define the work that we are privileged to do.

Sexual Healing

People get a little weird about hospice. People can also get pretty weird about sex. Put the two together? Well, most people don't put the two together, and really can't fathom that someone on hospice would still be sexual. It's as if a terminal diagnosis suddenly strips a person of every bit of identity and they become only "someone who is dying."

I suppose it makes sense that we do this as some sort of psychological defense. Dying is such a big thing to us that it becomes all-consuming. Granted, it's a pretty big deal, but for the person, it is still only one small part of all that they are, and ever have been, and still can become.

Multiple stories exist in hospice of patients of all ages who, for instance, had a lifelong dream of graduating from college, but were shy of completing their courses. Hospice staff will arrange for the receipt of an honorary degree, presented in style with cake, balloons, and a framed diploma.

Life does not stop until that actual nano-second when death finally does come. People do not cease to be who they are just because they've been given a new label of "hospice patient," or "terminal."

Hopes and dreams may come with a shorter expiration date; tastes may shift and priorities may realign; pain and other symptoms left uncontrolled, as well as overall fatigue, may in fact dampen desire. But in general, the biological, social, and emotional need for sexual, physical, and emotional intimacy doesn't simply go away.

One couple in their early sixties, young by hospice standards, came to the acute care unit where I once worked because the wife's metastatic breast cancer was advancing and her symptoms were not yet well-controlled enough for her to go home. She had been in the hospital for over a week and then came to stay with us until she felt well enough.

Her doctor was satisfied that her pain and nausea were finally being managed with just the right combination of medications. Sometimes, it takes quite a bit of trial and error to find that combo, especially when we take into account their desire to remain as awake and alert as possible to enjoy what time they have. We let the patient and family guide that balancing act based on what's most important to them.

She was feeling more like her old self, again. Her doctor indicated she would likely be able to go home in a couple of days if the current regimen continued to work. The last thing we ever want for a patient is for her to go home, experience a "pain crisis" and have to turn around and come right back. Pain is a lot easier to manage when we stay "ahead" of it with a consistent and workable game plan. If we do get "behind it," it can be a lot harder, and take a lot longer, to get the pain back under control. Her medical team was being proactive in trying to get her stable enough so that once she went home she could stay there until she died, which was her greatest wish (aside from not dying just yet).

I walked in the room and found the couple seated; she was in the bed and he was in a chair next to her. They were holding hands as they watched television. He stood up in gentlemanly fashion when I entered. I glanced up and saw they had been watching the local news. They told me it was their ritual at home to watch the local news followed by Dan Rather. She told me it felt nice to be some place that felt, "a lot closer to home than the hospital."

Acute care facilities, which are sometimes called hospice houses, used to be where people "went to die." Some still believe that's what hospice is—a place one goes specifically to die. As hospice care has advanced over the last four decades, most takes place wherever that person calls home, whether a private residence or a skilled nursing facility where they've lived for some time.

Hospice facilities now are most often designed to do immediate symptom relief and then get the person back "home" as soon as possible. Research shows that's where most people want to live their final days. Thanks to hospice, the number of persons able to do so is on the rise, but we still have a long way to go.

These hospice facilities are usually built with the comfort of the family in mind. Larger rooms, nicer furniture, fold-out couches, DVD libraries, rows of books and puzzles and games, a small fridge and micro-wave, a common activity room and play area, etc. all created to feel more like home for everyone involved. They are warmer and calmer and quieter, and usually lack that "hospital" smell many people fear.

After introductions and handshakes, he returned to his seat. His long cowboy legs in his creased and starched Wrangler jeans stretched out in front of him with his white socks sticking out of the ends. His boots were at the foot of her bed.

I asked how they were settling in, and he blushed a little at his socked feet, but grinned and commented how much nicer it was "away from all them beeps and whistles…though the hospital nurses were a little cuter."

She grinned and mock punched him in his arm, stretched out as it was over the armrest of his chair and the rails on her hospital bed and then bent at an awkward angle to reach her hand, of which he had yet to let go. They were incredibly sweet with each other and acted exactly as they must have when they met and fell in love as high school sophomores almost 50 years before. It was precious to see.

Noticing his arm, I showed them how to lower the bedrails so he wouldn't have to stretch and contort to be near her. He commented that he had sat exactly that way in the hospital for eight days straight, and she teased that she thought his body was stuck in that position.

I reassured them that we were glad his boots were off and that we wanted them to make themselves at home, "This whole place was designed to give you exactly that freedom. In fact, so long as it doesn't hurt you," I said, nodding to the wife then turning to the husband, "you're welcome to crawl right up there in the bed beside her, because by the way you two act, I'm guessing at home you sit a little closer than this to watch Dan Rather. You just may want to put the rails back up once you're there so neither of you falls off!"

You could see the uncertainty on their faces as they looked from me to each other to the space beside her in the wider than average hospital bed the facility chose to use. When we are out of our element, we often feel hesitant to take up space and act as we might otherwise when left to our own devices. The "rules" become engrained in us, and doubling up in a hospital bed clearly sounded to them like breaking a taboo that would prompt some sort of Nurse Ratched from the hospital four miles away to personally drive over just to scold them for their lack of decorum.

It was clear they wanted to be closer but "the rules" were getting in the way.

"Look," I offered, "you two clearly adore each other." I turned to the wife, "And you're here to feel less pain so you can go home. I'm betting that being near that tall drink of water will help almost as much as your medicine. If you don't mind my asking, how long has it been since you've had private time together, anyway?"

They started telling me their journey—breast cancer in the early 1980s, long and hard treatment, cancer free almost two decades, and then returning with a vengeance and spreading. From the time of her most recent diagnosis 12 weeks before, their lives had been a whirlwind of trips to specialists, scans, experimental treatments (given her young age), etc.

It soon became clear that this was not how they wanted to spend their last weeks or months together. By then, the symptoms were in full swing, and they had not seen home in weeks.

They were sad, but they were clear, and they were obviously in this together. After several breaths of silence, I reflected back to them, "You made the decision to stop seeking a cure because you wanted quality for whatever quantity you have. Please let me encourage you to not let anyone do any-thing to put one more inch of space between the two of you than you want or need."

I guessed at their next hesitation, remembering his gentlemanly blush at my "catching" him in his sock feet, "In fact, I have some paperwork to do and really need to just sit and do it for, oh, say, an hour and a half or so? We can't have locks on these doors in case a patient needs immediate help, but if I sit in my chair five or six feet down the hall from your door and tell the staff I can't leave until YOU open it again, I can guarantee you no one will get past me to come in until I do."

I waited patiently, but questioningly, for their response. Another slight blush, but also sweetly sophomoric grins flushed their faces. I started to leave, turning one last time to say, "Just please don't forget the bedrails, and don't forget to come open the door eventually or else my family will wonder why I'm not home for dinner!"

He winked at me, and nodded his wide-grinned thanks, and she laughed, taking 20 years and 12 weeks off both their faces.

I made it home for dinner. Over the remaining days they were with us, we eventually got around to talking about their faith and other things they needed to discuss, but not once were his boots anywhere but the foot of her bed nor he anywhere but snuggled up right beside her between those hospital rails, her head resting on his solid shoulder.

They looked exactly as I imagine they must have looked each night on their loveseat as Dan Rather joined them in the final hours of their daily ritual.

Brazilian Dancer

I want to know if you can be with joy, mine or your own;
if you can dance with wildness and let the ecstasy fill you to the
tips of your fingers and toes without cautioning us to be careful,
to be realistic, to remember the limitations of being human.

—from *The Invitation* by Oriah
(www.oriahmountaindreamer.com)

She was a young mother, a beautiful Brazilian woman in her late thirties. She was full of life despite the cancer that was now everywhere. She was horribly emaciated and weak. As her body tried to slip away, in the large room of the family-styled acute care unit, her spirit fought to live. She would just be about to drop off to sleep, and quite possibly death, when she would, by sheer force of will, jolt herself awake and raise herself up and out of her hospital bed.

She would proclaim passionately in her beautifully accented English, "I want to dance, I want to rollerblade with my son." Then she would grab the closest hand and say, "We have to dance." Exhausted, her slight body and determined heart would drop back into unconsciousness on her hospital bed.

Her young husband and the three young women who were her best friends, so close they called themselves "sisters," pulled me aside and said, "We don't think she gets it that she's dying. Shouldn't we tell her? We don't want her to miss the chance to say her goodbyes and we don't think she really understands."

I was a young, wet behind the ears chaplain full of verve and vigor and anxious to serve, I took their request to heart. I was determined to do my "due diligence" and help "guide her through her denial," so she could have a "good death."

The family stepped out to give us privacy.

I was the only one in the room the next time she awakened and bolted upright in bed. As we sat knees to knees, I gently tried to assess what she understood from the doctors about her condition. I slowly worked to nudge the conversation toward the truth.

Finally, she leaned over toward me, teetering precariously since she could barely sit up without falling over. She took my hands in hers and said lucidly, "Chaplain, my denial is the only thing I have left. Please don't take that away from me."

I had to swallow the lump in my own throat before I could speak, and then all I could say was, "Yes, ma'am." Over the next several hours, we took turns, her young husband, her sisters, and I, holding her up and dancing with her until moments before she died.

As a trained therapist, I knew better than to assume that I knew, but it is so easy to fall into thinking that we know...I just thought I knew what she needed. But she knew. Thankfully, she had the wisdom to tell us, and not let me rob her of the journey she deserved, her way. Thankfully, we could hear her.

Two A.M. On-Call

They had declined chaplain visits. It was two o'clock in the morning and I was on-call. The nurse contacted me and said, "I've given him enough meds by now to knock out a horse, and still for hours he's been wrestling and thrashing and moaning. This pain is spiritual, not physical. Can you come?"

I arrived at the patient's home and spoke with his wife of almost 40 years. He lay in a hospital bed in the middle of their living room. Everyone was there—their young adult children sat vigil by their father's side. There was nothing left undone that they knew of. They were an open, honest family who used very down-to-earth language.

Remembering they had declined spiritual care services, I asked, "Do you know what, if anything, your husband believes comes next after this life?"

She looked a little embarrassed and said, "I'm…I'm not sure," and then told me their story. Both had been raised in a very conservative faith tradition that preached, "…hellfire and brimstone," she said. They each experienced it as harsh and destructive, so they left organized religion in their college years, taught their children they were, "loved by G-d and to be loving to others, but beyond that we never looked back."

I considered this for a moment, then asked, "Is there any chance some of those childhood images of G-d are coming back to haunt him and he's afraid?"

Recognition lit up her face and she lifted her chest in a stunned intake of awareness as she turned to me and said, "Oh my gosh. That's it! Will you talk to him…please, and tell him it's going to be ok!?"

I put up my hand, as if to ward off the idea, and apologetically reminded her, "That's not what we chaplains do. We're not prescriptive, telling people what to believe. We help them sort through their beliefs and find their own answers. He's not responsive, I can't…"

"I don't care!" She stepped toward me with desperate intensity. "You go in there" she pointed at the living room, "and you tell him whatever you have to and let him know it's all going to be okay…Please!"

Conflicting standards and ethics rattled in my head as I simply agreed and said, "Yes, ma'am."

I walked slowly toward the living room, collecting my thoughts. The family stated they wanted to give us privacy, and went together into a back bedroom. I guessed they also needed a break from the hours of watching him struggle. I knelt beside his bed as he thrashed, twisting the bed sheets around and under him as he did. The rails of the hospital bed kept him from falling and the nurse had the bed lowered almost to the ground, just in case.

His moans and sighs seemed tortured, but he hadn't been able to speak for days, the family had told me. Nothing seemed to calm him, and this had gone on for many hours through the afternoon and entire evening.

In healthcare, we act and speak as if the patient can hear and understand us. It is both a sign of respect to always treat the patient with dignity, as well as an acknowledgment of the brain scans at the end of life that my medical colleagues tell me indicate the last senses to leave us are smell and hearing (http://dyingmatters.org/page/being-someone-when-they-die).

I sat cross-legged on the sunken floor in the middle of the comfortable living room, next to the head of his bed. "Hello, Mr. Jones. I'm Carla, one of the hospice chaplains. You and your wife have a beautiful family. She tells me you were raised in a conservative faith tradition, as was I, but that it wasn't a good experience for you. And I get that."

His eyes remained closed, but his head turned slightly my direction, his agitated movements and groans beginning to slow.

"I wonder if some part of you is scared that you're about to go meet a very pissed off G-d who's ready to make you 'toast'. I don't know about you, but I've come to believe in a G-d who loves you just as much as you love those grown babies in there, and who says, 'There is nothing you've done, and nothing that's been done to you that will make me stop loving you'.

"My best hope and prayer is that when you step from this life into the next, you'll be greeted by a G-d with arms open wide who beams at you and says, 'Welcome home, son. I love you, and I've missed you.'"

Immediately his body relaxed and his loud murmurs were replaced by the sound of his first deep breath in over nine hours. I called for his family, who ran into the room and gathered around as he took one more last big, deep breath that washed out of him in a great sigh.

We all knelt there in stunned silence at the rapid turn of events after so many hours of painful witness of his struggle. And then finally, his young adult son—this tall, muscled, dimpled 28-year old baby boy—said into the silence, "Son of a bitch, I swear he just smiled!"

And he was. He was absolutely beaming.

Did the medicines finally take effect? Did he hear what he needed to hear? We'll never know. But the experience has lasted with me ever since, and the family later explained to me that just seeing their husband and father calm and content for his last 40 seconds on earth made all the difference in their grieving. After nine long hours of watching his tortured grappling, they knew he finally died in peace.

I tried to use his belief system to address his spiritual pain. But I never could have done so had a nurse not recognized that the pain she was witnessing and trying to treat could not be touched by narcotics. I believe we must help all disciplines and families better understand and recognize the necessity of tending to spiritual wounds as part of treating the whole person. The more we understand, the better able we will be to treat the whole person, and by extension, tend to the needs of the family and prevent unnecessarily complicated grief and suffering for them, as well.

This—and so many other reasons just like it—is why I am extremely humbled and grateful for this work we get to do in hospice.

Hank

I rescued my border collie Hank (yes, like the cow-dog!), when he was about seven months old. He was so terrified when I first got him that he spent much of his first year on his belly with his ears down and tail tucked, terrified of everything. He was not socialized to humans or animals and didn't know how to play. I had to teach him the "down prance" that dogs use to communicate, "Let's play!" Shortly after I moved to Austin, I decided to take him kayaking for the first time.

So many things still scared him that I wasn't certain how he would do on the wobbly kayak. I was fully prepared to be flipped and dunked, but he jumped right on the boat and settled in like he knew exactly what he was doing! At first we floated around in a shallow area so I could be sure he was okay to go into the deeper main river.

Before long, we came across a family swimming in the clear waters just below the dam at Barton Springs, (a famous natural swimming hole in my beloved Austin). The youngest girl wanted to pet Hank, so her mother held her up to him so the five-year old could reach him from his nest on the front of the kayak.

Now, Hank is affectionate, but I had never seen him respond as he did. First, he licked the little girl a few times on the nose; then he stretched as far as he could off of the boat to make contact with the mother. He covered her surprised face with gentle kisses. I watched him continue to kiss her and said, "Wow… Hank…," and was about to call him off because you would have thought she had Alpo smeared all over her face the way he was licking her!

But before I could say anything else, I realized the mom had big tears in her eyes. And I saw that she had plenty of room to back up if he was bothering her, so I waited.

She took a deep breath, and when she could speak through the tears blending into the rivulets of river streaming down her body, said quietly, "Our dog died this morning, and he must sense it. Thank you, Hank. Thank you…"

I just kept quiet and let him do the ministering, as he and the woman loved on each other. She hugged him and stroked his soft ears; he collected her tears, giving them a place to be held.

When we eventually said our goodbyes, the woman let out a deep breath that seemed both a bit of resignation and relief in the midst of her tears. As Hank and I paddled away into deeper waters, I had to wonder, If dogs can be so completely open and sensitive enough to notice the pain of others, why can't we?

Hank has no letters behind his name, no chaplaincy or social work training to speak of, and yet he did far more than I ever could. That's because he saw her pain and was with her in it. He offered no existential discourse about the nature and meaning of suffering and, even better, no worn out clichés or theologizing words such as, "He's in a better place."

He was just with her. It was that simple. He offered whatever love he could, and it was more than enough. May we remember to be open to the tender places in those around us and use whatever simple gifts we have to offer them a moment of peace. I promise you, it may not feel sufficient since we want to "fix it and make it all better," but it truly is more than enough.

PET THERAPY
My "Accidental" Discovery

I had not intended to start working Hank as a therapy dog—yet. I was still working to rehabilitate him from whatever abuse and/or neglect he experienced before he found me when he was about seven months old. I was serving as a student pastor at my home church in College Station, Texas and, as I walked from my car to the church building one summer morning, a thunderstorm was brewing, whipping the few huge early drops just starting to fall literally sideways.

Suddenly, a handsome little red and white border collie ran straight to me from the adjacent field, across the parking lot, and wedged himself between my knees. He was trembling and whimpering pitifully, tail and ears down, but he licked my hand as I reached down to hold him long enough to disentangle our legs before I tumbled over him.

No one was in sight and a new clap of thunder sent him bolting in circles, terrified. With no apparent "owner" nearby and the storm hovering in that pregnant pause right before the bottom falls out of the sky, I whistled once and walked to the building. It took no more encouragement for him to come with me.

Once in the office, he expended all his energy, struggling to get as close to me as he possibly could. He whimpered and shook pathetically the entire time. Then all 30 pounds of him wound up in my lap as I searched to find the number for the animal shelter. They took my number and his description and offered to take him, but he was such a beautiful boy, I was afraid someone would lie if they caught sight of him and claim him for all the wrong reasons. After all, red and white border collies, called "merle," are pretty rare.

The shelter staff registered all the necessary information, and then Hank spent the rest of the day in my lap. When I got a call asking about him at the end of the day, my heart sank. But it was a young college guy who had found Hank, as he named him, running loose in the neighborhood earlier that very week and he admitted he knew nothing about dogs.

When he learned that I had rescued and rehabbed one border collie already, whom I worked as a therapy pet, and understood this amazing but quirky breed, he offered for me to keep Hank. I was thrilled because I had fallen in love on sight. He squeezed himself between my chest and the steering wheel on the way home. My first purchase for him the next day was his own cushion and seatbelt for the car!

My first border collie found me in a similar way. I was a ropes course instructor at a treatment center run by the local mental health authority while I worked on my first masters in Psychology. A stray dog was about to be shot by the maintenance man of the property because she kept chasing and even killing the ducks in the pond. When she made her way down to our camp, I sat on the steps of the porch with bologna slices in hand and spent what seemed like hours waiting for her to trust me enough to come close. I tantalized her with a piece thrown a few feet away, inching her closer and closer to me. When the smell finally over took her fear, she slowly crawled up to me, tucked in low to the ground, stretched out as far as she possibly could, and gingerly caught the edge of the slice in her teeth. When I didn't let go, she relented and came closer to get more, accepting my light touches.

The camp was called Wilderness Challenge, so I called her "Chally," and the name stuck. The kids loved her. She was also about seven months old when we found each other and was a brilliant dog. The breed is incredibly easy to train and she made me look like the "Dog Whisperer."

From the beginning, she would gravitate toward the shyest and most socially isolated kids who stayed at the camp for two to seven days at a time for various intervention and treatment programs. They would tell her to sit, and she would sit. They would tell her to shake, and she would. They would tell her to speak or give kisses, and she would do both. When a child would delightedly exclaim, "Miss, LOOK! Look what I taught your dog to do!" I would congratulate him or her for being so good with animals, and encourage the youngster to show the rest of the group what he or she had "taught" Chally to do. This would earn the child instant credibility, respect, and inclusion in the group. I watched it again and again and was blown away each time.

I was still leash training her, because like most border collies, she had a ton of energy and was unusually strong-willed for the breed, which lead to some nearly dislocated shoulders for me, at first, as any movement triggered her herding instinct. By this time, I was working as a Qualified Mental Retardation Professional for group homes and had to stop by the workshop where the residents who had graduated out of public school could practice work skills. Chally was with me for some reason as I ran errands, and the staff encouraged me to bring her in.

One of the residents, a 72-year-old man with multiple health difficulties in addition to his cognitive impairment, used a walker. He asked to walk Chally for me. Having instant visions of a cartoon version of this client flying "arse" up over his walker as Chally took off to chase a squirrel or bird, I declined. But he insisted, and so we compromised. He could "walk" Chally so long as I held onto the leash with him.

As soon as he put his hand on the leash, something shifted in Chally. He moved his walker forward, taking a small step; Chally took a small step, stopped, and looked up at him, waiting. Clop clop of walker legs, shuffle shuffle of slow and unsteady feet; step, stop, look up, wait. As they did their dance, I realized my hand was no longer on the leash. I had stopped halfway down the walk and just stared in astonishment.

For a moment, I thought, "Hey, what the heck!? Where was this dog yesterday when a piece of lint flew too close to you and you yanked me almost off my feet?" But somehow, she just knew. She knew he needed a lot more patience and gentleness, and she had it to give in droves. Once inside the workshop, the clients flocked noisily around her. She sat and accepted the well-intended grabs of her ears and tail and whiskers as I helped everyone understand to be gentle with her. Then I saw one hand stretch out from a young man in a wheelchair. He wore a protective helmet on his head, an indication he suffered from violent seizures and could not risk another head injury from a knock on the floor.

Chally leaned closer to the wheelchair to meet his reach. His hand quivered from the effort of slowly stretching out his fingers, drawn into the shape of a ball and curled into his palm from muscle spasms and atrophy. When his fingers were about three quarters of the way stretched out, he moved his arm stiffly back and forth to stroke the coat of her neck and along her back.

Mystified, the occupational therapist looked up at me and asked, "Can you bring her back every Tuesday and Thursday from 3:00-4:00 pm? We haven't seen him stretch out his hands that far in months and have a heck of a time getting him to do his exercises" (to keep his hands and wrists from completely drawing up against his inner forearms).

I knew I had stumbled onto something important, researched training programs, and eventually got Chally certified through the Delta Society. Whenever she "worked," she knew it, and was on her best behavior. The instinct to protect those weaker or in more need was written into her DNA, and maybe even her soul. She was a special dog and I miss her greatly. But thankfully, she was still with us the day I brought Hank home, scared, lightly crying, crawling on his belly with his tail and ears down in a sign of submission and fear.

He didn't know how to play with animals, people, or toys. His first toy was his Tupperware water bowl, which he chewed on while lying beside it lazily one day. When it dumped over on him, drenching his head with water, he shook off and, after a confused second of looking at it, trying to decide what he thought about the whole event, he finally grinned, picked up the now empty bowl and took off running in circles around the yard.

Chally helped me help Hank recover and learn tricks in that first year. And I think, when I wasn't looking, she whispered instructions to him to "pass the baton" so he could take over her work when the time came. Thank you, Chally. For everything. You helped raise not only Hank, but me, as well. I love you and I miss you.

By the time I was working as a hospice chaplain, Hank was still a little skittish of loud noises and sudden movements, not a good trait for a therapy pet. A traumatized dog can turn anxiety into inappropriate behavior, including aggression. Hank happened to be with me as I made one last stop for the day at a skilled nursing facility in a small town outside of Austin. I gave him a quick potty break before I made a quick stop inside and left him in the car on a very cool and cloudy day.

One of the certified nursing aids saw me and asked, "Before you leave, will you bring him by room 402?"

"Oh, I'm not working him, yet. He's not quite ready for that."

"Ah, that's a shame. She's a huge animal lover and just got here a couple of weeks ago from her home. They doubt she's going to be able to go back home and she had to leave her four dogs behind. It would mean the world to her."

Exactly how does one say "no" to that? So we followed her to the room, with the smells and sounds echoing off the slippery tile floors leaving Hank not so certain he liked this field trip.

Once in her room, I shut the door to decrease the noise—for his sake. As we turned, the patient, a tall and slender woman in her late seventies, weakened by a stroke from which she was recovering, saw us…or, saw Hank. She gasped delightedly. I introduced myself and Hank and we walked to be by her bed. "Oooohhhhhh, just look at you! Come here, baby," she said, patting her belly. Hank looked up at me, questioningly, knowing he wasn't supposed to jump up on people.

"It's ok. Up!" I commanded, and patted the bed rail, expecting him to place his front paws there and get closer so she could reach to pet him. Instead, he leapt like a rabbit and landed sprawled out across the woman's belly and chest, burying his face in her neck and wiggling in close to give her kisses.

The patient and I both exclaimed "OH!" in stereo; me out of surprise and fear as I tried to grab him back so he wouldn't hurt her; her out of total relief and ecstasy as she burst into tears and threw her arms around his slight body.

I looked to the aid and the personal caregiver, both who sat with the patient and knew her condition better than I did, and also knew if this was safe for her, who nodded reassuringly that this was ok. All three of us, in tears, turned back to the two snuggled up on the sterile white sheets in front of us, having a great big ole love fest and oblivious to the rest of us in that moment.

I slid the sheet up a bit to protect her fragile skin from accidental tears by Hank's nails, and just sat back and let them stay lost in their own little world. Hank whimpered soft sounds of excitement and she spoke lovingly to him in sweet tones. I swear they knew exactly what the other was saying.

They laid like that for as long as I could possibly delay. When they finally parted, I promised to bring Hank back, but when I did, I learned that the woman, in fact, recovered enough to go home to her own four four-legged loves. I'm not sure if a little vitamin "H" (Hank) provided the relief and motivation to make that happen, but I like to think that it did. Even if not, it did make her time of challenge a little bit easier to endure.

I've worked Hank as a therapy dog ever since, and we've worked on clarifying the "up" command! That day? I'm glad we hadn't gotten around to that, yet, and I'm glad the universe knew far better than I did what needed to happen, for all of our sakes.

Last Minute Forgiveness

I thought that perhaps they were just a more reserved family who did not show affection as outwardly as might others. The daughter was there almost daily. She and her mother said little to one another. When they did, there was warmth. However, I don't believe I ever saw them touch.

Then the mom took a sudden turn. Something happened, perhaps a stroke. According to our hospice nurse, the mother went from talkative at the lunch table with her friends at the nursing facility, to slumped and non-responsive. When I arrived, the nurse was sitting on the floor beside her bed, which was lowered almost all the way to the floor for safety.

The nurse (like so many hospice caregivers) is intelligent and practical with a very caring heart. She knows when to step in and take charge for the sake of a patient's care, and when to sit back and let things unfold. She has a strong sense of self that can be exerted, but also is deferential enough so as to not need to exert herself into a situation. It's an often-elusive balance, which she walks well.

I sat on the side of the bed opposite this nurse. My dog, Hank was with me that day and after nudging the hand of the patient with a kiss hello, took his post on the floor beside the bed and me. The nurse and I quietly sang in harmony some of the old hymns from the patient's church that we knew she loved. The nurse monitored her condition all the while, making certain she was comfortable. We both waited for the woman's daughter to arrive.

The patient's wishes were very clear—she wanted no heroic measures taken and wanted to only be kept comfortable if her condition changed. Fortunately, she had spelled it all out very clearly in legal documentation with her family and her doctors' knowledge and agreement.

When the daughter arrived, she stood for a long time in the doorway, barely coming into the room. She asked a few questions, absorbed the answers, and then asked the nurse if she should arrange to have her daughter join them. Given that the patient was in the "active" stage and it appeared her systems were shutting down quickly, the nurse agreed it would be a good idea if the granddaughter wanted to be there.

"I think she needs to be," the daughter said quietly, eyes still on her mother. Then she stepped out into the hallway to call from her cell phone. When she came back in, the nurse began to back away from her place on the floor near her mom's head so the daughter could come be closer to her. "No, no, that's okay, really!" the daughter quickly motioned my friend back into her place. "I'm okay, here."

I asked if she wanted privacy or company, and she asked us to stay.

So we sat quietly as we had been, humming a few more hymns here and there. The daughter finally sat in a chair a few feet further into the room, but still several feet from the bed. Hank looked at me, getting permission, before he walked over to offer his head on her knee for petting. She sat and stroked his soft red fur absently as she looked at her mother, no evident tears, just reflective.

She received a text that her daughter, the patient's granddaughter, was on her way. "She's in the midst of her mid-term exams. I was hesitant to bother her, but I think this is important," she said. Then she remained silent.
With a look to each other, my nurse friend and I silently agreed that what felt right was to give space, not ask, and wait. We held the patient's hands, placed a cool rag on her fevered forehead and cheeks now and then, and sat contentedly.

Her breathing continued to be ragged. Although she seemed comfortable, for the most part, the labor of the body learning to stop breathing can be a challenge. It wasn't quite to the point of seeming to need medication, but it was on the borderline and noticeable. .

Another text, "She's almost here." The daughter seemed anxious now. We waited.

The granddaughter arrived. She was a younger version of her grandmother and mother's elegant beauty. As she stepped into the room, this youngest of the three generations, burst into tears. Her mother met her just inside the door as it closed, and held her daughter. She patted her head while she cried and cried and cried, never taking her eyes off her grandmother as her chin rested on her mother's shoulder.

The initial onslaught of tears released a bit of their intensity, and they moved together further into the room, arms still around each other in long-practiced affection. They were both transfixed on the grandmother's form, as were the nurse and I.

The moment the granddaughter walked into the room, the patient's breathing instantly relaxed until it was even and calm. Something had shifted and there was no more labor. The change was palpable.

The granddaughter finally spoke, "It's like she did that for me." She stepped a few feet closer to the bed and said to her mom, "Do you think waiting for me was the closest she could get to an apology?"

Her mother nodded her agreement.

My friend and I still remained silent, allowing the encounter to unfold on its own with no outside pushing in any way.

A new type of tears began to wash the granddaughter's face. They seemed less hot and angst-filled; still painful, but more like tears of release.

With her daughter's head on her shoulder, and her hand still patting the young one's long brown hair, the mom began to explain: "When I was a child, my mother was my best friend. We adored each other. And then, when I turned five-years-old, something happened. My mother turned on me. She seemed to despise me and put me down, comparing me with her friends' and our neighbors' daughters and all of my friends. I was never good enough from that point on and all she ever did was criticize me.

"I lived with it and got through it. I decided to let it go and move forward. When my daughter was born, she and my mom were the best of friends. They did everything together. It was the mother I remembered, but had not seen, since I was a small child. It was bittersweet, but I was grateful that at least my daughter was going to get to have the mother that I once had but then lost.

"Then, my daughter turned five-years-old, and my mother turned on her, exactly as she had with me. To this day, we don't know why, but I was determined to not let my daughter be hurt the same way as I had. It was hard enough on her to not understand why her best friend suddenly 'went away.' For the most part, I kept her away, and made it clear to my mother that she would never be allowed to speak to my daughter critically if she wanted anything to do with either of us.

"We saw little of her after that, and even though we lived in the same town and I kept in touch, and have watched out for her care, my daughter has rarely seen her the last fourteen years. I simply wasn't going to put her through it, and mother never asked about her."

As we talked, they moved closer, and the patient relaxed further. My nurse friend and I inched slowly back to make room. Finally, we stood and stepped back to the far wall to give room as daughter and granddaughter sat on the floor at the bedside and took her hands, "It's okay now, Grannie. I'm here. It's okay. I love you."

"We're here, Mom. We're all here, now."

They sat like this for the next ten minutes as Grannie's breathing continued to even and relax and then ceased. We stepped out to give them privacy. Hank stayed behind with his head on the granddaughter's knee as she explored the hands and hair and soft wrinkles of a face so like her own, much as she might have done when she was a small child with the Grannie who had been her best friend.

There were no words for my friend and I once we were out in the hall. It's something you experience and wonder if you're imposing or projecting your own needs or wants onto the situation and translating it to be something so you can feel okay. I'm always open to that possibility. But sometimes, you see grace at work in ways that you just cannot explain, nor do you want to.

Whatever it was that happened, daughter and granddaughter received the healing they had needed for many years, and their experience of grief actually ended on that day, rather than begin. They had mourned her loss way too long. On this day, just for a few moments, they got her back, and then were able to finally let her go.

Re-Storying

I speak and write a lot about the stories we tell ourselves. I also talk about "re-storying." I know that my own on-going journey has involved letting go of the stories I used to tell myself, and leaving room open to consider something new.

We often tell ourselves that people are suffering and sometimes we are correct. It's also possible for us to project our own discomfort onto them, because we simply do not understand. So we have to pay attention to what is really going on, sit with what we see, and consider what information there may be that will help us better support the patients or loved ones for whom we care.

"Ms. N." moved her fingers in a certain way that made no sense to us. Then one day, one of the data entry clerks at the facility where she lived saw this and said, "Wow, she's doing 10-key, and she's fast!" In talking with her family, we learned she actually was a whiz and used this skill for many years in her job.

So the activity coordinator at the facility got her an adding machine. Engaging in an activity that was familiar to her made her so happy. This skill had given her a sense of financial security and value and meaning for most of her life. Replicating it lessened wandering behaviors and diminished the incessant "shadowing" of staff.

She no longer looked at me with haunted eyes and said, "I don't know what to do." What at first seemed like only nonsensical movement finally made great sense to us, and thankfully, we finally "got it" so we could support her. Just a simple shift in the story...

I spent weeks trying to figure out what "Mr. S." was doing when he moved his fingers in a winding motion, then later threw his arms over his right shoulder and then out in front of him back and forth a couple of times. His movements were unsteady, and a little hard to follow. Finally, I recognized the motion of tying flies and the figure 8 pattern for casting in fly-fishing. In speaking with his family, we found that he was an avid fisherman, taking every spare moment or vacation to "go be outsmarted by the trout," as he used to say.

Any time he could get his hands on papers, he would also shuffle those around repeatedly. His wife informed me that his other great passion was his time as an architect, and that he loved drafting.

As his dementia progressed and he could no longer be so precise in his work, she said he began to sit in his office for hours and file and re-file and staple and hole punch and clip paperwork, shuffling papers. She said it seemed like it helped him feel like he was still working. So the facility found an old drafting table and we got manila folders and notebook paper he could staple and file and draw on to his heart's content.

We also got some old bits for lures, (minus the sharp hooks, of course), so he could wind and tie and manipulate and feel them even as his vision significantly declined. More stories, more understanding, and thankfully more peace for Mr. S. as he smiled and wound and cast and drew and shuffled delightedly.

I learned that "Ms. B." was an incredible cook who loved everything about food. When she could no longer speak coherently, I would go into her room and turn on the cooking channel—Rachel Ray was her favorite! What she seemed to most love was for me to sit in the recliner next to her while she lay in bed after lunch. She held and patted my hand, smiling and giggling the entire time, as we watched Rachel Ray.

She oo-ed and ah-ed at the sizzles and steam as onions stir-fried and garlic caramelized. She tried to speak, but her brain could only manage "word salad" (words that are either not-discernible or are strung together in-correctly). It didn't matter. Her entire demeanor said it all. So I commented on the smells I imagined were coming from the pan and she sniffed the air exaggeratedly, made a "yummy" noise, and then giggled at her joke.

It was a new way of being with people that I was learning; new stories where once I told myself there was "nothing" they could do and how "miserable" that existence must be. But I was seeing contentment and even joy, especially when we could really take the time to see.

I grew up in small rural faith communities in the South. I sat next to many a piano teacher or pianist during my earliest years and there was just something about the incredible flourish of the extra keystrokes these women would add in that still gives me chill bumps today. It's a unique sound not just any musician can muster.

I was told Ms. Y. had played at her Southern church for decades. Her dementia had advanced to the point that it was uncertain whether she could still play. I asked the facility administrator, a dear friend of mine who knew Ms. Y. well, and she just smiled and said, "Oh yeah, if you can get her on that bench, you'll see!"

It took little coaxing. Once on the bench, she sat up taller than she ordinarily could in her wheelchair. Fingers that sometimes fumbled with her fork stretched expertly across the keys. She looked at me and questioned, "What key?" I smiled and joked, "Alto."

With a huge smile and a nod that said, "I can manage that." She played one note, then one a bit lower, and launched into an introduction of the hymn, using full five-finger chords flying all over the keyboard, in exactly the key I needed to lead the hymn! I clapped and burst out laughing in joy and amazement. Did I mention she had no music in front of her?

There will come a day when this is no longer possible, but when we tell ourselves a story about what persons with dementia cannot do, we miss the stories of what they still can do!

"Ms. N." crawled around in the corner of her room fussing with and knotting herself up in the bedspread she had drug off the bed and onto the floor. She surrounded herself with the tissue boxes and bottles of lotion she'd also pulled off the shelf and moved those around in the little nest she had made for herself.

Her daughter, who worked in the medical field, struggled to watch what seemed to her to be a tremendous lack of dignity exhibited by her mother. She grieved at the loss of who her mother once was.

"Look at her," she bemoaned, "she's rooting around on the floor like an animal! This is not my mother." Despite staff and family members' repeated attempts, Ms. N. refused to stay in the bed or recliner, and continually pulled her pillow and blankets to the floor with her to sleep, or be quite busy as she was this afternoon.

I reminded the daughter that persons with dementia often lose spatial sense and that their equilibrium can be impaired, leaving them disoriented by patterns on the floor that may look to their brains like holes in the ground or leave them feeling dizzy. I wondered aloud if the patient could be experiencing a fear of falling, such that the floor felt safer than the bed or chair.

The daughter appeared to consider this, and relaxed a bit. A simple re-framing or shift of our perception can sometimes make all the difference between something feeling traumatic and making rational sense.

I asked the daughter how her mother dealt with stress throughout her life. With absolutely no hesitation the daughter answered, "Vodka and chocolate!"

We laughed, and I said, "We'll see if the doctor can do something about the former, and I'll be glad to supply the latter if our nurse says it's safe for her. What other ways did she use to cope in her younger years?"

"Well," the daughter reflected, "she did always go for long drives in the country, and she cleaned. When we kids came home, we found everything pulled out from the closets and piled on the beds. Charlie Rich would be blasting on the 8-track. We kids would just turn around and walk right back out, because when she was stressed, she got on a cleaning tear and you might as well just stay out of her way!"

"She cleaned?" I asked, curiously, raising my eyebrows in question and then looking from the daughter toward her mother who sat on the floor, with two tissue boxes clutched in one hand and a bottle of lotion and a bed-spread grasped in the other.

Just to make sure, I reflected to the patient, "Ms. N, you're very busy."

She replied, "Yes, yes, yes…gotta make the bed, gotta make the bed, gotta clean up. Lots to do…"

After a moment of silence, I said, "I wonder if your mother is deal-ing with her internal stress in the same comforting way she has for decades, since chocolate and drives and vodka aren't handy to her anymore. It just looks a little different to us now than it did to you back then. I wonder if, instead of a lack of dignity, this is exactly what she needs to do to maintain her internal sense of dignity and control as she works out her fears?"

As we watched her mother "clean," it was as if the glasses on the daughter's face really did transform to a new lens. This was actually her mother, doing what she had always done, just maybe without Charlie Rich in the background. She was coping with the stress of the changes in her life in the only way that still remained available to her.

Her daughter left that day greatly relieved, seeing her mother in a different way—the old story, made new again.

Research demonstrates that engaging persons with dementia in activities that once gave them a sense of meaning can significantly decrease distress and "acting out" behaviors. It seems to lead to a greater overall sense of well being for persons.

It can be easy to overlook those who can no longer claim their space in conversations, the workforce, or group dynamics in quite the same way. But if we listen, if we ask about the stories, and as we learn about the patient through their loved ones and facility staff, we can discover who they were, and look in different ways to find that part of them that is still there. We learn what gave them meaning, what activities gave them the greatest satisfaction, and how they dealt with stress. It can be hard to see sometimes, and it may take a bit longer to look at them with a different lens, but it is worth it.

Holding Space

I am passionate about this work. I'm even more intent on teaching others, professionals as well as patients' loved ones and acquaintances, to just be with those who are suffering. I'm certain that's no surprise at this point in the book!

It's hard to do, often because we fear saying something "wrong" or because of our own discomfort and fears that lead us to shy away from being with grief and pain. The first can cause damage if words are misguided. Words are powerful because they can invalidate, minimize, or in many ways disregard the person's pain. They can even unintentionally inspire guilt. Yet to say nothing, and to not be present, is to leave persons feeling abandoned, which can hurt just as badly, if not more.

I had a brief medical scare in the fall of 2012 that turned out well, but it was interesting to watch others' reactions and notice the way people can "work their own stuff out" on someone who is in any form of crisis. I was given unsolicited and usually unwelcome advice that felt condescending, overwhelming, or left me feeling unseen and unheard when it was far off the mark of my situation. I heard lots of opinions about how I "should be" handling things. I was given clichés and theological platitudes that left me feeling hurt and angry, and often blamed.

Thankfully, this grief-thing is my field and I could see it all for what it was—well intentioned. But the misguided things we do to protect ourselves, and each other, from feeling fear or pain are not helpful. As a professional trained to notice and also to avoid using any of the emotional defense mechanisms we humans can employ to protect ourselves from a real or perceived threat, I recognized (and even "resembled") some of those techniques.

I experienced from the receiving end of the situation things that I have said or done professionally, or personally, when I was a rookie. I've even made these mistakes as a seasoned counselor. Fatigue, stress, and just being human can illicit from any of us well intentioned but inappropriate comments. My professional training allowed me to feel compassion for the most part and not take things personally, but it wasn't always easy.

If there is any pain that we fear or have experienced and not fully processed to healthy resolution, then we are left even more vulnerable to committing such infractions against others. When we encounter a situation with someone else that reminds us of our own vulnerability to that pain or negative experience, we can sometimes make light of, deny, or brush it away because we may feel threatened by their pain and want it to go away. However well we process our own pain is exactly how well we will be able to respond to the pain of others (or not!)

I had to remember that truth when folks said things to me that were not what I needed or wanted to hear. I also felt guilty for the times I had committed those errors and realized how truly sad and lonely it feels to be on the receiving end. I began to compile a list of the "Well-intended but clueless things we say."

The following year, I was asked to do a national presentation on grief, loss, and bereavement (a fancy word for the grief process) and knew immediately what I would share. Folks want to know what to say and how to help. I presume goodwill, so I do not believe anyone set out to hurt me, they were simply fumbling through this life thing like all the rest of us. I believe if we talk about the discomfort, and challenge ourselves to let go of our verbal security blankets, we can find a different way and do this whole "support" thing even better! We just need some better tools.

So I wrote: "How Not to (Unintentionally) Say Something Stupid—BE-ing with Those Who Are Suffering." I have presented it several times. In short, we need to remember that this is the other person's process, not ours, so we should not impose on another's journey. We do not have to, need to, or get to fix it. We can find space within ourselves to just BE with what is, most often in silence.

If this process is theirs and not mine, and if what is happening isn't really from or because of me, then where DO I get to be in this process and what DO I get to do?

Most often I simply get to hold compassionate space with them while they talk and find their way through the pain (as we heard earlier from Herbert Adler's words comparing therapeutic listening to dialysis). Not everyone can accept being so much less than "the hero" who saves the day. It is definitely a temptation to fly in with cape flapping and make ourselves feel better by taking on that role. Persons often fail to see the power they have by simply being with another in a compassionate way without needing to do anything more than that.

I think part of our struggle is that we believe suffering "should not" happen, and we want to take action to correct it. We protect ourselves from constant fear by telling ourselves on some level that tragedy, illness, and the like will not/should not happen to us. It is a defense mechanism—one that has gone awry. It leaves us vulnerable to disillusionment and resentment when suffering does cross our doorstep.

It also makes it hard for us to witness the suffering of others without wanting it to quickly go away. "I feel uncomfortable watching you suffer, so I want you to hurry up and feel better so I won't have to face the fact that suffering happens as a natural and often unpredictable part of life. I don't want to feel anxious and out of control."

Aside from accepting that life isn't pretty and perfect, we can also alter our negative perception of suffering. We would love to learn and grow by eating cotton candy and riding ponies at the fair, but that isn't how growth happens. As E.H. Chapin is quoted as saying, "Out of suffering have emerged the strongest souls; the most massive characters are seamed with scars."

We can trust that great things can come even from the worst of pains.

Most of what I try to teach (and increasingly learn to practice myself!) is to just hold the space. To be with what is and bring a sense of calm and peace first to ourselves and then, hopefully, to the room.

Holding is so primitive. A healthy mother instinctively knows to hold her child. If she does not, the child will fail to thrive and will essentially wither away despite ample food, shelter, and hydration. We are designed to need each other. We are pack animals, after all.

It is what we most need and yet it is often what scares us the most— the connection that can comfort pain. We want to reach out and yet it brings up our own "stuff."

We can provide presence, sit with silence, follow their lead, avoid clichés and theologizing, and as one wise grief counselor stated, "Never start a sentence with: 'Well at least…' because no matter what follows you are minimizing the griever's feelings."

This is something we can learn to do over time. The best way is to practice showing up, allow yourself to make mistakes, apologize, and then keep getting back up on the horse. In time, that delicate art will be refined, and on most days you'll find you're able to just be. As the old adage goes, "Don't just do something, sit there!"

Waking Up

As I've said, sometimes it ain't all that pretty! Not everyone arrives at a place of readiness at the same time.

The ongoing process of watching a loved one decline, and all the challenges that come with that journey often wears down family members who are in town. They see the patient's incremental changes and hear their expressions of fatigue with trips back and forth to the hospital, more tests, more complications, and more losses. "She's tired. She doesn't want to do this anymore, and I honestly can't blame her."

Out of town loved ones, even when kept well-informed by siblings with reports of Dad's worsening condition and reports from his doctors, can have a more challenging time wrapping their heads around the reality. It's a natural defense the psyche uses to protect us, and it makes sense. No matter how hard we try to accept the news we hear, not seeing it makes it challenging to comprehend. The experience lived daily is much harder to deny.

Rather than the continual downward trajectory and daily suffering in-town relatives see, out-of-town loved ones come back to visit and are alarmed with what appears to them to be a drastic stair-step of change for the worse. It is not uncommon for the shock to show up in accusations that care has been lacking and demands for aggressive action. Add to this shock the internal struggles many feel with guilt or regret when they cannot be closer and more helpful and involved, and it can get pretty messy.

Emotionally and physically weary from constant caregiving, the accusations feel like salt in the wound, especially if the in-town relatives are feeling put upon and unsupported. "I've been here every day for her treatments and done everything I know to do, with almost no support. I've seen her cry and beg to be done with all this. And now they come in and question me, and the decisions I've had to make alone? It's so unfair."

It would be nice if skeletons in the closet and old baggage and triggers that lie within and between us would simmer down and behave in times of crisis. Sometimes, that happens. Folks are able to see what's important, put aside squabbles and differences ranging from, "Mom always liked you best," to "Why did Dad abuse me and not anyone else?" and find a way to work together in a supportive manner.

Other times, however, the gremlins with which families struggle eat a pound of chocolate, drink a case of colas, and pump up on steroids 'til they are running amuck and creating as much havoc as possible, mowing people down in Barbie cars down the toy aisle. So when we say that caring for and supporting families is as much a part of our work as supporting patients, we aren't kidding.

As my spiritual director says, "No good guys, no bad guys, here. Just humans doing their best to figure out this messy thing called life." Whatever it looks like, it's part of the process and each person deserves the space they need to find their way in their time.

But here's the tricky part—when those journeys collide, whose needs takes precedent? Mediating needs can be one of the more difficult tasks we healthcare staff face. Grandma doesn't want the oxygen and keeps knocking the tubing off her face, but Granddaughter repeatedly puts it back on. Dad bites down on the spoonful of applesauce his son keeps forcing between his lips and doesn't let go, clearly wanting nothing to do with eating.

It's what we know to do to feel like we're not "giving up." I encourage family to do whatever they feel like they need to do so that later, their grief will not be complicated by doubts and questions and regrets. The bargaining portion of the grieving process can sound like, "If only we had…," and "Why didn't I…?" We don't want to set them up to wonder and struggle any more than necessary.

We also don't want to allow what we know to be uncomfortable, or even harmful interventions from family, to take away the peace and dignity that the patient deserves. So we educate them about the end of life process while helping them talk through memories of their loved in a way that helps them process their grief.

We tell them that when a person starts to refuse food at the end of life, it can actually be a sign that their system can't process it anymore and putting it into their bellies will cause them to bloat and have pain. We remind them that the nasal cannula for oxygen is purely about comfort in the final days and will rarely make or break the moment when a person's body is finally ready to die. It can, in fact, dry out the sinuses and cause more discomfort than relief, and the noise can be quite distracting, making weakened voices hard to hear.

Again, we help them find other ways to "do something" to nurture their loved one. We show them where and how to massage feet and hands, how to lotion dry and irritated skin, to cool a fevered brow, and how to watch for signs anything we are doing is actually irritating the patient rather than helping.

It's a process of acceptance and letting go. Our bodies and brains are hardwired to survival. Letting go of that takes time and a lot of pushing back from life before we can often come to terms with reality and say, "Ok, enough. I get it."

What a tricky balance it can be, for us all.

She took him home from the hospital for the last time, alone. Helen and Tim fell in love after being introduced by co-workers. She said this was a second marriage for them both, and their children were not pleased with their new respective stepparents, so they did not come around much.

They had lost contact with their friends as his illness progressed and they spent most of their time pursuing aggressive treatment around the state. When they came home the last time, she said she wasn't ready to answer questions, deal with company, or "share" him and this precious time with others.

Our nurse met them at the hospital, as he was being discharged to his home and onto hospice services, and followed them there to help make the transition smoother. She spent the late afternoon and early evening making sure he was finally comfortable. Our social worker sat with Helen to give her space to talk as she made sense of this final drastic turn of events.

When I arrived to visit the next morning, our Certified Nurse Aid (CNA) had just left from giving Tim a bath and he was sleeping comfortably in his bed in the master bedroom just off the open living room. The house was quiet, except for the occasional creak of farmhouse hardwood floors as we walked to sit on the loveseat under the window near his bed, talking in soft tones.

Helen shared their story and about what a wonderful man he was. She spoke haltingly of her beliefs, her fears, and then shared more about their lives together. Everything poured out in a jumble.

"Our first marriages were so bad that we clung to each other when we found such a good thing. We were inseparable and didn't want to lose one moment. I don't know how to be 'me' without him, anymore".

As she talked, I noticed a new sound in the quiet house as his breathing shifted markedly in the bed nearby. Though I'm not a nurse, we're trained to be able to notice and report changes to the nursing staff, but we must be careful about diagnosing what is happening physically, especially to the family lest we make a mistake and cause undue distress.

His breathing appeared to be that of someone with minutes to hours left to live. At first, it deepened, lengthened, relaxed, but grew louder with audible sighs. Then with each breath he took, there was a period of apnea (lag time without taking a breath) of several seconds in between.

I excused myself for a moment, explaining I needed to go back out to my car to get something and called the nurse to tell her what I was seeing and hearing. She diverted her schedule and headed that way immediately. It was going to take her about an hour to get to the rural home. Per both the nurse's and social worker's assessments the previous day, they agreed the wife was far from being ready. I went back inside to walk with the wife as she found her way, at a rate much faster than she was ready to take.

After being away from home and physically in pain, to finally be at home in his own bed, comfortable and clean is often all that a person needs to relax into his death. It's not the "morphine" or any negative euthanasia myth some believe about hospice.

It's purely about the relief that comes from comfort and familiarity and closure that allows the adrenaline of pain and anxiety to slow down long enough to let the body heave a relieved, Ahhhhhhhh…finally! We can relax and let go and let this happen.

He had been home barely more than 12 hours. He was ready. She was not. She was leaning over the bed curiously watching his breathing. She looked over at me questioningly when I walked back in. I just breathed and stood at the foot of the bed and waited to see what she was ready to handle.

"Right after the CNA left from giving him his bath this morning, he fell into a deep asleep", she said, "But now…something's different."

I watched as her wheels turned. "It is markedly different. I called the nurse to let her know of the change", I said. "She's on her way."

Brow still furrowed in confusion and concern, she sat back down on the loveseat. I joined her there and was in the midst of asking her where their admission packet (to hospice services) was. I explained that we included in there an educational booklet that helps families understand what to expect as the end of life approaches. In the busyness of their trip home the day before, and the sheer exhaustion of everything they were facing, she had not yet read it.

We were new to each other and I wanted to tread lightly to give her the space she needed to come to terms with what her eyes said on some level she recognized, but they also pleaded for more time to live in the fantasy and not "know" what was happening.

And then, as we opened the booklet between us to review, I heard the silence as his next period of apnea went on for more than a few seconds. He had been clear that no heroic measures were to be taken and they both chose to sign the Do Not Resuscitate order before even getting into the ambulance for the transport home.

The statistics on the success of CPR and other methods of resuscitation on young, healthy bodies in the hospital with expert staff and specialized equipment around are still quite small. For an older body compromised by illness and already failing, the physical damage and emotional trauma it causes are, most often, far too extreme to be ethical or wise.

Her head jerked up at the lack of sound. "He is making some very fast changes, Helen," I observed. I was about to encourage her to be with him and say whatever she wanted to say to him, when she got up and leaned over him. When it was clear he wasn't breathing again after a good 45 seconds, she jostled him gently, calling his name. He began breathing again with a bit of a start, and she relaxed, sitting back down.

She resumed sharing their stories, ignoring the booklet and my attempts to speak. I hushed and let her talk. Everything about her screamed, Not yet; I'm not ready. Please! I followed her lead.

Then, another long period of apnea ensued. Again, she shook him and woke him back up. When she looked up at me, it was clear she finally realized what was trying to happen. "He seems ready," I said.

"I'm NOT", she cried.

"I hear you," I affirmed.

She continued to talk, now watching his chest constantly. His lapses in breathing came more frequently and it took her more energy and pleading each time to jostle him back to breathing again, "Tim, come on baby. Wake up for me. Please! There you go…" as his breathing resumed, appearing more shallow each time.

The cycle continued as she wrestled with her feelings and his process, pushing him to stay. Finally, I placed a hand on her arm as she sat down once again, "For now, you can do this as long as you need to. But you know that at some point he isn't going to be able to come back to you, no matter how much each of you want that, and you'll need to let him finally have peace. I trust you to know when that time has come. Until then, do what you need to do so you can feel as if you've said and done everything you need to in order to feel ready."

It was one of those hard, "grey area," moments when whose needs take priority isn't quite clear. I truly wanted to press her to stop and let him go, but instinct said she needed to do this. Everyone will likely find the line in different places. It is the art that exists in the midst of the science. I am called to advocate for and protect patients. I am called to serve the needs of the family and allow everyone their respective journey. No small order.

Finally, as she sat again after waking him again, she looked at me, "I know I need to stop… I know I'm being selfish."

"What do you need to be able to let go?" I asked her. She looked helpless and lost as she held her own breath and faced the tide that would soon make her efforts to plug the dam beyond futile.

"Soak him up," I encouraged. "Memorize every touch, every smell, every line in his face and hands. Find whatever it is of him that you need to hold onto, so you can let him go."

The nurse arrived, and I went to let her in. We stood just inside the doorway of the bedroom. Without looking up, Helen said, "I know it's not rational, but now I feel like if I stop doing this, I'm killing him. But all I'm really doing is robbing his peace. He's given so much to me, it's not fair for me to do that."

With that, she leaned down, dropping tender kisses on his cheeks and lips, holding his face in her hands and stroking his hair and brow. With one last, "I love you. It's ok. I'm ready now," she left the bedside and came to stand between the nurse and me. Arms linked around each other, we watched silently as he slid back into a long period of apnea.

She vibrated with the strain of holding herself back from running over to shake him and beg him to wake one more time, and she grasped onto us as if we were anchors to help hold her steady as she rode out her emotions and the moment as the tide finally carried him away into a peaceful death.

As we stood there in the uninterrupted silence, Helen shared that Tim was always the more logical of the two, more practical in his ways of seeing things. "He gave in to me, quite a bit, knowing I just needed more time than he did to come around."

After many minutes of waiting to be sure, the nurse finally asked Helen if she was ready for her to pronounce his death. Her vibrating and clinging had eased, and a sense of calm had found her. She stood taller, and nodded her consent. More silence followed until the nurse gave the final word and declared the official time of death.

Turning to me, the wife said, "I didn't think I was going to be able to do that. I know it wasn't pretty to watch, but thank you for giving me time."

She was right. It wasn't pretty to watch. It was quite an anguishing hour. I hurt for her. I hurt for him. I was early enough in my career that I was still building that trust that now carries me a lot further, and a lot longer as people find their own way in their own time; and that what I think needs to happen is what I am needing to happen.

Since this process isn't about me, I get to let go of that, and only step in minimally. The more I grow, the more I learn the less I truly need to step in. As one old school nurse said to me, "If they think they couldn't have done this without us, we haven't done our job. It's not us. We just remind them what they already know."

Helen and Tim had long navigated their relationship of patience and pulling and finally coming around. This was one last gift they could give each other—he to her of the time she needed, she to him of finally coming to terms. Who was I to interfere with that process?

Gentle guidance sparingly given, a listening ear, ethical education, and sitting with our own "stuff." That is the process to which we in hospice get to slowly, eventually, wake up.

If I Don't Say I'm Sorry

The truth is that our finest moments are most likely to
occur when we are feeling deeply uncomfortable, unhappy,
or unfulfilled. For it is only in such moments, propelled by
our discomfort, that we are likely to step out of our ruts and
start searching for different ways or truer answers.

—M. Scott Peck

When someone is going through a challenging experience, our
natural instinct is most often to say, "Oh! I'm so sorry…" It seems the kind
and even socially acceptable response to another's pain. A few years ago,
however, a wise teacher gave me a beautiful example of an alternative that is,
I believe, far more compassionate, but not necessarily easy.

I was struggling during one of those life challenges that really gnaws
at your gut and will stay with you forever, for good or for ill. As I spoke with
my spiritual director one day she said to me, "When you're hurting, if I
don't say, 'I'm sorry,' it doesn't mean I don't care." It occurred to me in that
moment, that I truly had never, even once, heard her say those words.

"When I say, 'I hear you,' that's me saying 'I care'. But if I don't say,
'I'm sorry', it's because I'm not."

I was quite taken aback by this. I opened my mouth a few times to
respond, then closed it again each time, not quite sure what to say. Confusion
and borderline hurt were likely written all over my face.

In answer to the questions I couldn't articulate she said, "I know
when you're hurting, that you're teachable. Pain impels us out of our comfort

zones and toward greater health, compelling us to grow. Because I care, I can never be sorry for you to have that experience."

I said, perhaps a little sarcastically, "Gee…um, thanks?" But I got it. And I still experience it as the highest form of caring from her, as well as her trust in my ability to make it through tough times.

Many people ask me how I do this work. If there's time, I'll share that story with them. It's changed the way I see situations. I can feel for someone going through difficulty or suffering, and I can care about their struggle, but because I trust them to find their way, and because I believe that even the most challenging times can also result in great gifts, I feel less of a need to "fix" things for them.

I may not like what they're going through; often, I just flat out don't understand. But I trust the process and I have less of a need these days to rail against "what is."

While I do not propose to believe in a deity who causes or prevents bad or good, I do believe in a deity who shows up and says, "Well, this stinks. How can I bring as much good out of this as possible?"

It is how I handle the question of theodicy—where is G-d in the midst of suffering, or how can an all-powerful and all-loving G-d allow evil to exist? It's what works for me. I don't pretend to know that it's' right. I don't need to. I just know that it's where I find meaning and peace in the midst of the crap we do sometimes see in our work.

Experience has taught me that something I believed at one time was the best thing in the world can change into a difficulty in a second, and the things I most resented in the moment often resulted in some of my greatest gifts.

All of this has given me the humility to know that even when I think I know, I do not know. And when I'm really certain that I know, to think again. Through all of it, my personal faith that great gifts can be found in any circumstance helps keep me grounded and calm…well, most of the time!

The Queen

It's important that we do not come to this work needing it to make us feel okay about ourselves. In my boundary trainings, I begin by asking, "First, we know not to take money from patients and families, right?" The group usually laughs and nods. "And second, we know not to have sex with them, right?" Louder laughs and bigger nods follow.

Smiling, I add, "If you don't know numbers one and two, come see me afterwards, because that's a problem! Today, we're going to talk about those boundaries we don't discuss at dinner parties. They are the subtle, seemingly innocent, but much more insidious boundary breeches, which I believe precede all the rest. Those are the emotional boundaries we cross when we come to our work needing something from the interaction, wanting it to go in a certain direction so we can feel okay about ourselves."

I go on to explain that this circumstance occurs when we do not have our own lives and sources of support and care. As a result, we look to our work to "fill us up" rather than coming to this work already "filled" and allowing our work to simply fulfill us. It's a subtle but significant difference that can make or break our effectiveness and our ability to not burn out.

In the former case, I need something to happen in a certain way or need someone to have a certain experience, or to respond to me in a certain way. With that approach, the interaction becomes about me, what I need, and I lose my objective focus about our clients' wants and needs.

In healthcare, we break down boundaries this way: we do nothing for our own benefit at the patient's expense. When we approach our caregiving from a place of our own need, we unwittingly take advantage of patients and families emotionally, sacrificing their needs so we can tend to our own feelings.

In the latter and healthier case, we have our own lives, our own emotionally satisfying connections. We don't bring our "baggage" into the interaction, but instead allow ourselves to enjoy the positive connections, which can naturally occur as we walk with people on the journey they need and want. It's fulfilling and we appreciate it, but we don't need it to make us feel whole.

We can want certain things for them. Of course we don't want someone to feel pain: physically, emotionally, or spiritually. Of course we hope people will like us and that what we do will have an impact. But when we need those things, we become dangerous. And none of us got into this field to do harm!

I continue in the boundaries training by discussing ways we can protect ourselves—our colleagues—the patients and families who trust us. We can facilitate their process without the breeches mentioned while still allowing ourselves to be human and appreciate the connections we can make. I also discuss how to handle it when someone does, "get in," despite our best attempts.

No matter how diligently we work to maintain boundaries, some patients will inevitably trigger old stories, some positive, some negative, inside of us because they, in particular, resonate with us in some way.

For example, when I first began working as a hospice chaplain, I realized something was getting "stirred up" by one particular patient. We had good conversations as he worked to resolve business issues so they would not fall to his wife to attend.

He stated he realized he had done her a disservice by taking care of all their business and household finances and legal issues, because now she felt overwhelmed and unprepared to pick up the reigns he had carried for 42 years of marriage. "I thought that was my job, to care for her in that way, but now I realize I've handicapped her and it wasn't fair to do that."

He struggled to sort through his guilt, regrets, and worries for her. He questioned his legacy since his business was being rapidly sold to partners, with whom other emotional and legal dynamics existed. We talked through his beliefs about healing and hope and he started to find peace as he repaired many internal and interpersonal wounds.

None of this was necessarily unique. He was gentle and kind. He and his wife were sweet with each other as they "cleaned up" long-standing issues between them and used their faith to bring them closer together and cope with their anticipatory grief.

But I found myself wanting to avoid his room, sometimes waiting until late in the day to see him. I couldn't figure out why I was having trouble until I was documenting in his chart one afternoon and noticed his birthday: it fell very close to my father's in month and year.

Oh, his birthday is near my dad's, I thought...then realization dawned: Ohhhhh....his birthday is near my DAD'S! Instantly, a sense of calm settled over me as I simply acknowledged that his age and a few other similarities with my own father were triggering my own anticipatory grief about the fact that he, too, will one day die, and I'm not yet ready for that to happen. Conversations with him tapped into fears of my own grief and loss and I wanted to avoid that, so found myself wanting to avoid him.

Fortunately, this insight was enough to clear the way for me to have an easier time with this patient. If not, I would have had work to do to protect this man from my issues, which could potentially impact his care while putting me through an emotional ringer. If I couldn't get past it, it would have been my duty to refer him to another chaplain.

Still others remind us of ourselves, for good or for ill. One woman, whom I'll call "Martha," was called "The Queen" by those who cared for her.

She had been found on the streets, incoherent, filthy, and ill. She was admitted to a skilled nursing facility, where her hair was washed and cut away from where the tangles were hiding her face; long and curled-inward nails were trimmed; and hydration and medications were given to treat her delirium. At that point, the full weight of her personality came flying out with all its brilliant colors—and colorful, she was!

As she returned to health and mental clarity, answers came. She had been a professional in the area, working for years as a respected manager at a treatment center. As she retired and her friends moved one-by-one to be closer to family, she found herself without a safety net of relationships. Rejected and shunned decades previously by her own family, with no significant other or children of her own, she found herself increasingly alone.

Then she became ill. With limited resources and support, she went undiagnosed and untreated. Everything after a point was fuzzy to her memory, but her home and possessions were gone, so she took shelter literally under a bridge, where a network of our brothers and sisters who live on the streets kept her safe and alive as best they could until they could find help for her.

The staff at the facility that took her in was jubilant when they saw her full-blown, intelligent, and funny self come to light. That jubilation turned to great sadness as her blood cells and exam results told the rest of the story—it was end-stage cancer. Treatment was not an option. She did not have long to live.

"Telling her the news was one of the hardest things I've ever had to do," the nurse who took a personal interest in her case told me. "Here she was getting a second chance at life and a family to love her…"(the staff threw boundaries out the window in this case and adopted her as their own), "… and then to learn that she was dying…we both cried that day, sitting right here in my office."

They called hospice. At first, I'll admit to a bit of concern and slight judgment that the staff were taking this case so personally and had gotten so close to her.

Then, I met "The Queen."

She was ballsy, if you'll forgive the term, and quite brash. I knocked on the frame at the open doorway of her room and asked permission to enter. She was sitting up in her bed reading a book while simultaneously watching a news show on the television near the foot of her bed. She turned toward me, looking appraisingly over the rim of her readers and somewhat down her nose at me for a long time. I waited quietly just outside her door. It was one of those moments that you just breathe; let yourself be "sniffed out," and trust things to unfold however they will.

In a thick Northern accent, she bested any truck driver in the country as she spat out at me loudly and disdainfully, "Who the (blank) are YOU?!"

It was clear; I had one chance. In a millisecond, I made a decision, and without missing a beat I replied, "I'm your (blank)ing chaplain. May I come in?"

Feigning stunned indignation, she fired back, "You can't say that, you're the chaplain!!"

"I may be the chaplain, but that makes me no better than you, so if you can say it..." I let the rest remain unspoken and stood my ground with a raised eyebrow. I either just blew it or I was in like Flynn, I thought. I spoke a silent prayer that I hadn't severely misjudged and misstepped.

She erupted in raucous laughter, "I LIKE you! You can come in. You passed."

Whew.

Judge me if you will for using such language as a chaplain, but I will always prefer to commit such a "sin", if you call it that, than to be guilty of the sin of not meeting her where she was and in a way that honored what she seemed to need in that moment.

She told me of her life, her loves, her losses, her proudest moments as a teacher and manager and counselor. She explained that she could not stand pretension or disrespect, especially from those who were weak enough to need to puff themselves up to feel okay, often at the expense of others.

"People don't think anymore," she complained, "we're too busy running around being scared all the time and just spouting stuff without realizing what we're saying and jumping through hoops to try to get people to like us and get ahead".

We had forged an understanding.

"What are you up to?" I asked her one day as I entered her room.

"About 5'1'" and getting shorter every day," she retorted cheekily. "Now, ask me how I'm really doing, if you can sit for longer than five minutes and really give a rat's ass about my answer."

I smiled. The teacher was still teaching her students, whom she considered to be everyone within earshot. She barged right into that "buffer space" we seek to keep between ourselves and the patients with whom we work. She asked me to bring my family by to meet her.

I reminded her that we keep some separation between our work and professional lives for everyone's sake.

She was clearly not impressed, "Aw, hell! Life is too short and too precious and I ain't got that kind of time. Either we're real with each other or I don't have time for it."

I held that boundary, and others, but she got inside in other ways just simply by being so real, a hybrid of Archie Bunker and Mr. Rogers! I adored her as much as did most everyone else around her.

She frequently decided to have some fun with a person, messing with their heads to make them think. For instance, one time she asked an aid who took her drink order for lunch if they had any "diet water." She laughed as the confused young woman stumbled and stuttered and then went off to ask the kitchen if they had any! "That's my job, and I'm pretty good at it…," she bragged, "…at making people stop and think. That's what I've always been called to do and will do until the end." She looked at me and said, "Speaking of, have y'all decided when that's going to be, yet?"

I referred her to the nurse for medical questions, but asked her what she thought. "I think I'll know. I can already feel it coming."

We spoke about what she needed and wanted from her remaining time, and her conflicted beliefs about what came next after this life…if anything (she wasn't so sure). She was a devout Catholic, but questioned whether God would accept her.

As we spoke, she made it clear that she did not want a priest to administer the final sacrament or anointing of the sick. She asked me to do it. As a non-Catholic who tries to walk carefully between the lines of my job and the work of faith leaders along cultural and theological boundaries, I hesitated, but she was insistent. Not wanting to offend good Catholics, but also not wanting to offend her and her needs, I finally agreed.

It was almost impossible not to love this woman. Everyone did, once they passed her tests. Some, she put through the paces until they accepted her rules. Only then did she let them in. She could argue anything and her compassion and love were clear as the foundation of her passion, so she was hard to deny.

I knew this, so I stayed in close contact with my spiritual director and my team. I wanted to maintain good boundaries, even if they were stretched to their furthest limits by her, for both the sake of her good care and my own emotional protection.

As she reviewed her life (it's important to note that spiritual care counselors' and social workers' roles overlap a great deal, we just come at it from different angles), she spoke of her grief over the rejection by and loss of her family.

I did not tell her I related to this to some degree.

As we discussed what she wanted for herself for her last days, she grappled spiritually with her hurt and anger and grieved the nieces and nephews she lost, in addition to her siblings. We explored forgiveness and healing and her beliefs about each. We discussed how to find the space to both grieve what we experienced and perceived to be the reality of a situation while also letting go, just enough, of our hold on the story to find some sense of peace.

She prayed. A lot. She cussed. A LOT. Often, she did both at the same time as she wrestled with God about it all, from family to cancer.

She said she wanted the chance to see them one more time. I asked if she wanted the social worker and me to try to find them for her?

She pondered it for a long time and then said she would think about it and let me know.

Finally, she had her nurse call me to come see her. As I walked in and sat by her bed in silence, she remained still. When she finally looked up at me, it was the first time I had seen her cry, yet she also seemed strangely at peace. In an uncharacteristically soft tone, she said, "I've done too much work over the decades to heal from their first rejection to risk going through a fresh one all over again...and this time from a second and probably third generation. I just don't think I have it in me. As much as I want to see them, I can't handle one more heartache. I'd rather miss them and not know, than to try and then know for sure if they still hate me."

This is why we keep our boundaries. Everything in me wanted to argue, to encourage her to try, to push her to let me or the social worker "screen" them and feel them out and only get them in contact with her if they had moved to a more accepting place where she was concerned. But this was not my journey. It was not my risk to face. They were not my wounds to heal. They were hers, and hers alone. It was her "good death" and I had no business believing I knew better than she what she wanted, was up for, or could handle.

If I push to open up a can of worms with which someone is not prepared to deal, I set them up for failure. We make steps when we are resourced enough to do so. Until then, our resistance often has a protective purpose. She made her decision. She was clear, and she was at peace. I had no business pushing that.

The healing I wanted was for her, but also for myself. It would not have been fair for her to bear the weight of responsibility for vicariously repairing both of our old wounds. I could not let what I wanted to impose upon what she desired.

Somehow, knowing that this time she had made the choice where her family was concerned, rather than having a separation she did not want imposed upon her, she seemed to find some empowerment that healed the feeling of being a victim. She found her way to forgiveness and let go of the worst of the blow-ups and soul-crushing words she had experienced.

She found peace in her way, and she cussed a lot less as she prayed for them!

Many things especially endeared this woman to me, and I knew that this time…this death was going to be particularly hard on me. So I told my team, who already knew it, and understood; and I talked with my spiritual director who could help me process what I needed outside of her room so I could show up effectively and ethically for her.

Some just get in, and she had with me. The trick is not to be robots or perfect or somehow super human, but to be vigilant so that when it does happen, it doesn't catch us off guard and lead us to mismanage our care for them.

When the time came, her favorite nurse called to let me know. She declined suddenly into that comatose state many fall into as the body shuts down. The facility did a beautiful job of getting her into a room closer to the nurses' station so they could keep an extra eye on her. They also put her in a room alone, so she could have peace from the extraneous noises that often bothered her during her waking hours.

Honoring my promise, I brought the final prayers she requested I say over her before she died to her bedside. Cancer was taking her body, but it had never taken her brazen, crass, loving, humorous inner strength and zest for life. Seeing her this way was hard.

I made it my last visit of the day, since I was not sure how I would do. I'm glad I did. I was alone in the room with her as I finished the prayers, "And now in the name of God most Holy who created you (sniff, sniff) and the name of Jesus Christ who redeemed you (sniiiiiiiiiiffffffff), and God's Holy Spirit who sustains you, may you rest this day..." The final words should have been "...in God's eternal home", but the last words dissolved into sobs.

I've been in the caregiving field for over two decades. Not once have I lost it like that. I'll be honest, I feel pride at working hard to keep those clinical boundaries, so I felt a bit frustrated and ashamed at, well, being human, I guess. (That pride is definitely human, as well!)

I was trying to pull myself together to say the final words, when a very large and gentle hand slid over my shoulder, past my cheek, and held out a wad of sandpaper quality facility tissues to me. "Here, miss," came the voice of the sweet giant of a young man who had walked in behind me. He was one of the Certified Nurses Aids who worked with this patient, and he understood.

After I took the wad and nodded my thanks, since I could not speak yet, he just put his humongous hand on my shoulder and squeezed without a word for a long moment. I reached up to pat the hand of my hero in that moment and heard his own sniffle from behind and a foot and a half over my head as we stood together and watched this dear, incredible woman decide it was time to move on.

I didn't need to look to know that he was weeping, too. The entire staff was there for this woman whom they had claimed as their own, since no one else would. They protected her fiercely and loved her deeply. They would do anything for her. I took one of the dry tissues from the wad he had handed me, and gave it back over my shoulder to him. I wish I knew where he was now so he could come help teach my classes on being present.

A bit relieved by the release and the act of kindness and camaraderie, I finished the prayers; gave her a last hug; thanked her, and told her goodbye. She was also clear that she wanted to die alone. That was one request that the staff had a hard time honoring as they streamed in and out of her room all day, saying their goodbyes. But they did, for The Queen, who refused to play by any rules and was determined to teach us all so very much.

To Be Clear

I've attempted to state several times in this book that the end of life process isn't always a picturesque Norman Rockwell scene. Beautiful, poignant, profound, and touching moments certainly do happen and, they are largely what keep us going.

But I had a conversation with a colleague who cared for patients with dementia and who had read the abbreviated E-book version of *Hospice Whispers: Stories of Life* when it first came out. She shared honestly that, while she absolutely loved the stories and learned a lot from them, she said, "I came away from them feeling like I suck compared to you!" To be fair, she is still in seminary and just starting her work in this field and the learning curve is huge. Yet, I was saddened that this had been an unintended consequence of the book.

In that moment, I realized that she had not attended my trainings, and I had left out a crucial piece of information when writing this book that I often share when I present about dementia! So we sat over coffee and I filled in the gaps to share with her:

I am a raging extrovert and truly love engaging with people. I'm also an external processer and work well when the person with whom I'm speaking is engaged. I feed off of the energy of our interaction.

So when I would visit a patient who had dementia or was otherwise non-responsive, it would only be about five minutes before I was like a fidgety five-year-old in the bank, wanting to throw my head back in angst-filled exasperated boredom and plead, "Can we go home now, PLEEEAAASSSSEEEEE????"

I'm not proud of this. But it's the truth. I share this in training because usually 90% of the room will nod their heads in commiserating empathy. They get it, because they've experienced the same thing and usually smile and laugh in relief that someone is admitting it out loud. It's just flat out hard for the vast majority of us, as we're still trying to learn how to just be with people who, more and more as our bodies live longer than our minds are accustomed, do not appear present.

I knew I was doing a disservice to the patients, their families, the agency for which I worked, and even to myself! So I began to learn. I read books by experts such as Naomi Feil and watched videos of her and other dementia specialists such as Teepa Snow on YouTube, and read Tam Cummings' *Untangling Alzheimer's: The Guide for Families and Professionals*. I went to any presentation I could on dementia.

As I did, I found ways to sit still and quietly and to take the time to find the connection that doesn't always happen, but occurs far more often when I can slow down and enter their world and their "language." It began to feel more like a puzzle to unravel than a burden to endure, and I began to have experiences like those described in this book.

Whether a patient has dementia or anything else that decreases their ability to communicate in the way to which I am accustomed and which comes easily to me, they deserve me taking the time to slow down, seek out, and match the way that they can still connect.

As I sat down with my friend, the new hospice chaplain, and shared all of this, her shoulders instantly relaxed and she released her tension with a sigh of relief. I reminded her that these stories are moments taken from almost a decade of working with persons at the end of life.

I told her of the times that I sit for months on end with a patient with dementia, looking for a way to find a connection with them that sometimes never seems to come. I've no idea what is going on behind their often vacant expressions, so I cannot be sure, but I don't always come away feeling as if I have made some profound difference. I get to accept that just being there, in the best way I know how, and trying to offer compassion and presence with them, is enough.

I spoke of the days when I just don't feel like I have it to sit, when someone exhibits a behavior that I don't understand like confusion or agitation and I fear that I'm going to make them feel worse or that others will judge me for not being able to bring comfort instead of more stress. I get to let go of my ego and have some compassion for my humanness that wants to help and "get it right," but that also can lapse way too far into perfectionism, comparison with others, and self-judgment, thinking myself "less than."

Even further, I hate paperwork and, even though I teach documentation to spiritual caregivers, I will avoid it as long as I possibly can each day because it feels like such a laborious task. I can do it pretty well, but I also get tired and lazy and slide by in mediocrity, which isn't the way I like to show up for my work responsibilities.

I may call some families for weeks (or months) and never speak to anything but their voicemail with never a return call. It starts to get challenging making "cold calls," and feeling almost like an intrusive telemarketer, wondering if my messages to them are comforting because they know someone went to see dad or just one more annoying thing on their already overflowing to do list. So I find ways to offer for them to let me know if they want no more calls, which I won't take personally, and that I just want to do what is helpful for them. Then I get to make a judgment call if I still don't hear back and hope that I'm erring on the side of what feels good to them.

In person, some families or patients do not want to have one more conversation with a virtual stranger and have their own way of coping that does not involve allowing me to be present with them.

I make mistakes and missteps and misread a situation and bumble each day. I have days where I'm the one who feels like my friend and think, "I suck at this".

I sit with patients and families who do not get the storybook ending, the resolution, or the peace in any way that I can see. But those aren't really for my eyes, anyway. Sometimes, I just get graced to see them. It's their experience and I regularly get to let go of needing anything from the interaction, even affirmation that I'm doing something "right" or "helpful."

I sat for months with a patient whose mother had been a follower of Harry Houdini, whom I did not know had quite a following of faithful devotees. According to the story, as the patient understood it, Houdini had promised his followers that when he died he would find a way to come back and tell them about the afterlife as a means of reassurance.

This patient's mother promised her young son the same. After she died in his teenage years, "She never came to me like she promised," he complained with big tears in his 82-year-old eyes. "I've always wondered, what was so wrong with me that she didn't come to me and give me some sort of sign like she promised."

Abandoned by a dying mother, he clung to her promise, but then his sense of abandonment only deepened over the years and he never healed and now, at the end of his life, he was left with huge doubts about both his worth and the existence of an afterlife. Each scared him tremendously.

The social worker and I were each using the skill sets of our respective disciplines to try to help him find his way through his unresolved grief and renewed fears as he faced his own mortality. We coordinated weekly to support each other in supporting him. Before we saw him experience much progress or find much peace, he had a stroke and scans indicated he lost most of his reasoning capacity. We had to let go of needing to know if he ever found, or no longer needed to find, resolution for his feelings. Not easy. Not fun. But a necessary part of the reality.

As written previously, rallies don't always happen, patients don't always wait for everyone to gather around the bed and hold hands in resolution of grudges; realizations don't always come to which I am privy. I have to trust that life is just unfolding as it will and that each person can find their way and even find peace, meaning, and comfort in each circumstance no matter what it may look like. It's the only way to get through each day.

This book was intended to point to the rich gifts and experiences that punctuate what seems to the outside world as an impossibly sad job. My hope was to make death seem a little less scary, to make hospice just a little better understood, to help families and even patients feel just a little more prepared for what the process can look like.

But to be clear, it ain't always puppies and ponies. I am good at what I do, but I am by no means the best or wisest chaplain I know. This book isn't intended to be a made for television movie in which the ending is all neatly tied up with a delicate bow. So please, do not hold yourself as a patient, family, or professional caregiver to a standard that isn't real. We look for the gifts and beauty and perfection in the midst of all the messy imperfection and seek to learn from it all—the seemingly "good" and the seemingly "bad."

As artist Salvador Dali' said, "Have no fear of perfection—you'll never reach it." Thankfully, we do not need to.

Already Inside You

The greatest good you can do for another is not just to share your own riches but to reveal to him his own.

—Benjamin Disraeli

At the heart of good chaplaincy, I believe, is the call to be more about walking with people as they find their own answers and less about wanting (or needing) to reveal how much we (think) we know. I am not here to tell you how much I know.

I am grateful to have learned, and to continue to be learning, more than I would ever have dreamed imaginable from the patients and families and colleagues with whom I work. But even those lessons are not truly "mine." They have been borrowed and combined and refined from and for this work we are privileged to do, but none of it really belongs to me.

I simply wish to invite you to remember how much you know.

A writer and speaker whom I greatly respect is Paula D'Arcy. When she was twenty-seven-years-old, she survived the head on collision with a drunk driver that killed her husband and two-year-old daughter. Paula was three months pregnant at the time. After coming through her own "dark night of the soul," she found a deepened faith and openness to the light that exists in the darkness, and worked for years as a grief counselor. Her story has touched countless numbers and she now writes and travels to speak and lead retreats worldwide through her Red Bird Foundation.

When I read her words or hear her speak, something both stills and stirs deep within me. I feel the truth of her words in my bones, and part of me really wants to be her when I grow up!

I had the opportunity to visit with her at length one afternoon in her home. We shared stories and lessons from our respective journeys, personally and professionally. Paula has fully developed the art of, "being with what is," and gives no sense of needing things, or people, to be other than what or who they are. I asked her many questions, and she explored them with me, ever so gently and patiently and with this sense of respect for my wisdom that continually refused to accept a position as somehow "greater than" me.

I was beginning to speak more and more before professional groups across the country during this time, mostly about the material and lessons contained in this book. I felt like a "newbie," wanting direction from someone who had walked this path. She keeps a balanced sense of who she is without giving into the seductions to which those who stand before groups and receive accolades often, tragically, succumb.

I have seen first-hand the destruction that can occur when charismatic leaders do not bring their best and most grounded selves to their work, and I approached my new stages with excitement, but also trepidation.

I shared how uncomfortable I felt when persons came to me after I spoke and thanked me, sometimes gushingly, about how what I had said had touched them. I did not want to fall into the trap of believing my own press and seeing myself, or allowing others to see me, as the "sage on the stage" who knows all. I am confident, but I strive always to be mindful lest that confidence come across as, or even actually become, "cocky." Losing sight of the fact that I do not "know it all" would be dangerous territory to which I do not want to go, personally or professionally. I don't want to be "that person."

I am clear that whatever I share has been borrowed from others or gleaned from hard lessons that life has taught me. I try to remain mindful not to block the gratitude that others share with me, which would be disrespectful, but I also do not want to agree with the idea that I am somehow more "gifted," or better than others.

Through all of it, something greater than me has guided me and I hope to always remain open and teachable. Persons of faith often speak in terms of being, "only the vessel" through which the Divine speaks. My desire is to simply be such an open channel.

As I met with Paula, I asked a lot of, "How do you…" questions.

She sat quietly for a moment, then said, "Most often, I simply say 'Thank you.' But other times, if it seems appropriate and there's space to do so, I will say, 'If something I said spoke to you, it is only because it resonated with that which already exists inside of you. If it did not, you would not have been able to hear it.'" A buzz tingled under my skin. It felt right. Her words matched what I believed and felt but had not the words to convey.

A couple of weeks later, I conducted a one-day workshop with a colleague. Afterward, I had a conversation with an attendee who shared back and forth with me about what he thought and felt about this work. He told me the things in the training that resonated with him, and the things my colleague and I had shared with which he was struggling. Toward the end of our conversation, he began to express his gratitude and respect, and then enter that space that begins to feel uncomfortable for me by telling me how great he thought I was.

I shared the words Paula had given to me, "You know, a wise teacher I know told me that if anything she said was meaningful to me, it was only because it already existed inside of me or else I would not have been able to hear it."

He had been leaning inward, toward me, with his eagerness to thank me. But now he pulled back. He paused, seeming to think about this. He held his breath a moment, looked down, then back up, and his energy completely changed.

He stood up taller, beaming, his chest puffed out a little as he took in a deep slow gasp of realization. "Wow," he smiled, "that makes sense!"

Suddenly, the power dynamic in even the physical space and positions between us had shifted. He was no longer leaning into me, placing the focus on me. He was acknowledging and accepting his own wisdom, and appeared to take some healthy pride in the idea. I was not the "sage on the stage," nor was he the passive learner. We were just two human beings, learning from and sharing with each other.

It felt right. The pride and respect were reciprocal. Neither of us was robbed of or given too much power or dignity. It was shared. And the gratitude turned from that unilateral space of him thanking me, to both of us reverentially accepting that something greater than us both was present. We both brought ourselves, and all the lessons other teachers of experience and other people had shared with us, to the interaction. It was good and felt "clean."

As we do this work of caring for others, we are mindful that we keep clean boundaries so that patients and families are not asked or expected or even allowed to give to us, meaning we do not become one more burden patients and family members must tend to in the midst of their struggles. We do not come so they can make us feel good about our work or ourselves. We do not share our burdens with them.

But we also are not really "taking care of" them. They are caring for themselves. We simply get to have the gift of being present with them and helping them hear themselves and the wisdom that already exists inside of them. We can avoid dumping our problems on them. We can be clear that we are not there for them to care for us and our needs.

But we can also go even further, and continually be clear that we are not the "end all, be all," making them "be okay." They are doing this for themselves. We get the gift of being present as they do so and, as we hold that space with them, we receive gifts as well. We share the information, facts, and specialized knowledge we have gained from our respective professional studies and our work, but they also bring themselves and their truths.

Remember, anything we say and do that is meaningful for them is only possible for them to receive because something inside of them is already prepared to receive it. We've done nothing to earn it or make it happen. We can help make it possible by how we show up with them, but ultimately whatever good happens is not a work of our own doing, and they deserve the pride and dignity that comes from acknowledging that.

And so do you, my reader friend. If anything I have written here speaks to you, remember that on some level you already knew it, or else you would not have been able to hear it from me. If anything I've said challenges or offends you, I invite you to consider why that may be, especially if it elicits a great deal of energy from you. Perhaps I can learn from it, as well, should you choose to share it with me.

Regardless, whatever benefit may come, I trust that it is yours and hope that it sustains you to continue to bring the best of who you are to this work that we all do with each other as human beings: learning to show up, to truly see and hear, to hold respectful space, and to offer open-hearted care.

And so may it be.

To learn more about Carla's trainings and writings,
go to http://carlacheatham.com

Made in the USA
Middletown, DE
23 March 2019